A BUNCH OF AMATEURS

by Ian Hislop and
Nick Newman

SAMUEL FRENCH

Copyright © 2017 by Ian Hislop and Nick Newman
All Rights Reserved

A BUNCH OF AMATEURS is fully protected under the copyright laws of the British Commonwealth, including Canada, the United States of America, and all other countries of the Copyright Union. All rights, including professional and amateur stage productions, recitation, lecturing, public reading, motion picture, radio broadcasting, television, online/digital production, and the rights of translation into foreign languages are strictly reserved.

ISBN 978-0-573-11373-4

www.concordtheatricals.co.uk
www.concordtheatricals.com

FOR AMATEUR PRODUCTION ENQUIRIES

UNITED KINGDOM AND WORLD
EXCLUDING NORTH AMERICA
licensing@concordtheatricals.co.uk
020-7054-7200

Each title is subject to availability from Concord Theatricals, depending upon country of performance.

CAUTION: Professional and amateur producers are hereby warned that *A BUNCH OF AMATEURS* is subject to a licensing fee. The purchase, renting, lending or use of this book does not constitute a licence to perform this title(s), which licence must be obtained from the appropriate agent prior to any performance. Performance of this title(s) without a licence is a violation of copyright law and may subject the producer and/or presenter of such performances to penalties. Both amateurs and professionals considering a production are strongly advised to apply to the appropriate agent before starting rehearsals, advertising, or booking a theatre. A licensing fee must be paid whether the title is presented for charity or gain and whether or not admission is charged.

This work is published by Samuel French, an imprint of Concord Theatricals. Ltd

The Professional Rights in this play are controlled by Casarotto Ramsay Associates, Waverley House, 7-12 Noel Street, London, W1F 8GQ.

No one shall make any changes in this title for the purpose of production. No part of this book may be reproduced, stored in a retrieval system, scanned, uploaded, or transmitted in any form, by any means, now known or yet to be invented, including mechanical, electronic, digital, photocopying, recording, videotaping, or otherwise, without the prior written permission of the publisher. No one shall share this title, or part of this title, to any social media or file hosting websites.

The moral right of Ian Hislop and Nick Newman to be identified as authors of this work has been asserted in accordance with Section 77 of the Copyright, Designs and Patents Act 1988.

USE OF COPYRIGHTED MUSIC

A licence issued by Concord Theatricals to perform this play does not include permission to use the incidental music specified in this publication. In the United Kingdom: Where the place of performance is already licensed by the PERFORMING RIGHT SOCIETY (PRS) a return of the music used must be made to them. If the place of performance is not so licensed then application should be made to PRS for Music (www.prsformusic.com.). A separate and additional licence from PHONOGRAPHIC PERFORMANCE LTD.(www. ppluk.com) may be needed whenever commercial recordings are used. Outside the United Kingdom: Please contact the appropriate music licensing authority in your territory for the rights to any incidental music.

USE OF COPYRIGHTED THIRD-PARTY MATERIALS

Licensees are solely responsible for obtaining formal written permission from copyright owners to use copyrighted third-party materials (e.g., artworks, logos) in the performance of this play and are strongly cautioned to do so. If no such permission is obtained by the licensee, then the licensee must use only original materials that the licensee owns and controls. Licensees are solely responsible and liable for clearances of all third-party copyrighted materials, and shall indemnify the copyright owners of the play(s) and their licensing agent, Concord Theatricals Ltd., against any costs, expenses, losses and liabilities arising from the use of such copyrighted third-party materials by licensees.

IMPORTANT BILLING AND CREDIT REQUIREMENTS

If you have obtained performance rights to this title, please refer to your licensing agreement for important billing and credit requirements.

AUTHOR'S NOTE

Amateurs and professionals

A Bunch of Amateurs is a love-letter to amateur dramatics. It's a world with which both Ian Hislop and I are very familiar – from disastrous school productions to hilarious village hall Victorian melodramas. We also owe our writing partnership to the amateur stage – as a result of a truly terrible school production of *The Peterloo Massacre* Ian and I began performing revues and writing sketches. As we ourselves turned from amateurs to so-called professionals, we never forgot the excitement, terrors, passion and sheer fun of am-drams – along with the rivalries, bitchiness and pratfalls. If you want to see pomposity pricked – go and see an amateur production, in which the high and mighty have to play the lowliest parts, and career success gives way to acting ability. It is, like having children, a great leveller.

The story of the play *A Bunch of Amateurs* began in 2004, when we were approached by our old friend David Parfitt (a shy Oscar-winning producer) to look at a film script he had in development, which had stalled. Based on an original story by John Ross and Jonathan Gershfield, *Amateurs* was a fish-out-of-water tale set against the backdrop of an amateur dramatic production of *King Lear*, in which a failing Hollywood star arrives to create mayhem. We had, till then, enjoyed an amazingly lucky and varied career writing for some of the funniest people ever to appear on television. This was a departure – a film – and, moreover, a film in which a theatre had already expressed an interest. From the outset, the Watermill Theatre near Newbury had been keen on the idea of a play – but that was to come many years and many, many rewrites later.

Before then, we had the task of turning a terrific idea into a sellable cinematic script – and while we were comfortable working for radio and television, we had never actually written a film for general release. We were the amateurs. We had begun as sketch-writers. In the early 1980s we began collaborating on the satirical puppet show *Spitting Image.* Ian was fresh out of university and working at *Private Eye* magazine whilst teaching at a sixth form crammer. I had been working as a business journalist, writing extremely boring, chin-stroking articles about the future of the aerospace industry for *Management Today*. In my spare time, I drew cartoons – contributing first to *Yachting Monthly*, then *Private Eye* and *Punch*. When Ian got a call from *Spitting Image* producer John Lloyd, he suggested I come along to look at the pilot show. It was brilliant. We had a sketch in the very first episode (the Reverend Ian Paisley having an argument with God) but unlike the pilot show, the first series was not at all brilliant, and was slaughtered by the critics. However, by series three it was getting audiences of fifteen million (and critics were saying it wasn't as sharp as the brilliant first series!).

Five years later we were *Spitting Image*'s chief writers, commissioned to write twenty-five minutes of material a week. We reached the zenith of our career in rubber with the 1987 election show (broadcast live just as the polls had closed), with a parody of *Tomorrow Belongs to Me* from *Cabaret*, performed by Maggie Thatcher and the Tory cabinet. The song, recorded weeks before the election, happily proved to be right on the night; so we despaired and rejoiced at the election result in equal measure. We had also co-written specials for David Frost and NBC (a horrified US executive said, "Are you suggesting that President Reagan is an ASSHOLE?") – as well as UK one-offs: *The Sound of Maggie* celebrated Thatcher's tenth anniversary in power, and marked our first foray into the theatre. I dimly remember Maggie as Lady Bracknell exclaiming to Neil Kinnock, "A *windbag?!*"

But by then we were utterly burned out as topical sketch writers and running on empty. Ian was now editor of *Private Eye*, and beginning his career as a TV presenter and panel show contestant. I had packed in my job as a business journalist and was about to begin a career as pocket cartoonist at *The Sunday Times*. There was no obvious reason why either of us should carry on working together – except that we enjoyed it. So carry on we did. We wrote a TV play, *Briefcase Encounter*, for Maureen Lipman and the late Simon Cadell; a Radio 4 series, *Gush*, starring Martin Jarvis, Caroline Quentin and Felicity

Montague; and we were asked to write sketches for Harry Enfield's new eponymous TV show *Harry Enfield's Television Programme*. We came up with a character based on old school chums. He was called Tim Nice-But-Dim.

We were always lucky that *Private Eye*'s bi-weekly production cycle meant that every other week is an "off" week in which to write. So we were able to write for all series of Dawn French's *Murder Most Horrid* and had the joy of seeing our words performed by some of the best comic actors in the business, including Timothy Spall, Hugh Bonneville, Philip Jackson and, of course, Dawn herself. The episode starring the future Lord Grantham was directed by the infant Edgar Wright, who went on to film such comic masterpieces as *Shaun of the Dead*.

Lest you should think that it's a relentless joyride, I would point to the skip-loads of rejected scripts we have produced, the reams of unproduced treatments and sheds-full of receipts for ultimately futile "ideas" sessions in Clapham wine bars. Along the way there have been disastrous pilot shows, empty promises by producers and dashed hopes aplenty.

But then once in the bluest of moons we have written something of which we have been truly proud – such as *My Dad's the Prime Minister* for BBC1, with Robert Bathurst, Carla Mendonça and Joe Prospero; or Radio 4's *The News at Bedtime*, starring Peter Capaldi and Jack Dee; and, more recently, our BBC2 BAFTA-nominated World War One comedy drama *The Wipers Times*, with Ben Chaplin, Julian Rhind-Tutt and Michael Palin (also subsequently turned into a stage play, which premiered at the Watermill Theatre in 2016).

In the midst of this scriptorial rollercoaster ride of success and failure came the call from David Parfitt to have a look at the film script of *A Bunch of Amateurs*. We suggested some changes – with which David happily agreed, and suddenly we were plunged into writing a screenplay. Three years and countless rewrites later we were on the red carpet in Leicester Square, enjoying the unexpected honour of being presented to the Queen. Starring Burt Reynolds, Samantha Bond,

Sir Derek Jacobi and Imelda Staunton, *A Bunch of Amateurs* was chosen as 2008's Royal Film Performance. Her Majesty apparently enjoyed it so much that she requested a screening at Sandringham that Christmas.

The experience of making the film was to have a direct impact on the writing of the subsequent play. Whereas the film was written purely from the imagination, the play was based far more on our experience of working with a *bona fide* Hollywood star. Like our hero the former Hollywood legend Jefferson Steel, Burt Reynolds was looking to reboot his career. Like Steel, Reynolds was surrounded by actors more versed in Shakespeare than he. Like Jefferson, Burt had a problem remembering some of his lines. The words "I can do it with a look" saw a page of dialogue disappear on screen. So when the Watermill finally commissioned us to write *Amateurs* for the stage, we knew we could make it much richer and more realistic.

Writing for the theatre was yet another new experience, and meant tearing up the screenplay to produce a new script to reflect the story's theatricality: a smaller cast, but more Shakespeare, more am-drams and more jokes about Hollywood stardom – now that we'd actually worked with a "movie legend" in the tautly-honed flesh. That was a truly bizarre experience, which we've tried to capture in the play. A strange case of art imitating life imitating art. The Watermill production also featured a unique combination of professionals and amateurs – members of the community theatre appearing in key scenes to bolster the action. In reality, as in the play, the worlds of the amateurs and professionals collided.

As a piece about the redemptive power of theatre, *Amateurs* is more appropriate on the stage than on the screen. As our hero, the fading Hollywood legend Jefferson Steel would say, misquoting King Lear, "The play's the thing". And nowhere is the play more the thing, than when being performed by a bunch of amateurs.

Nick Newman

Produced by The Watermill Theatre on Thursday 22 May 2014 in association with Trademark Films. With the following cast (in order of appearance):

Jackie Morrison **Dorothy Nettle**
Michael Hadley **Nigel Dewbury**
Sarah Moyle **Mary Plunkett**
Damian Myerscough **Denis Dobbins**
Mitchell Mullen **Jefferson Steel**
Emily Bowker **Lauren Bell**
Eleanor Brown **Jessica Steel**

Director **Caroline Leslie**
Designer **Tom Rogers**
Composer **Paul Herbert**
Assistant Director **Neil Bull**
Lighting Designer **Tim Lutkin**

The action takes place mainly in the barn which the Stratford Players use for rehearsals and performances of their amateur productions. The barn has a door and a window. Throughout the play the barn will be transformed gradually into a stage set for King Lear. There are some scenes in the local bed and breakfast. Scene changes are accompanied changes of lighting and musical accompaniment of the Fool's Song delivered in various permutations.

lights by door all off.

CHARACTERS

Jefferson Steel – a fading Hollywood star who is arrogant, insecure, brash, gauche, demanding, vulnerable and ultimately aware of his own absurdity.

Dorothy Nettle – director of the Stratford Players and the moving force behind keeping the theatre alive. Her sweet and accommodating manner conceals her inner steel.

Jessica Steel – Jefferson's teenage daughter, who has been neglected by her Hollywood star father and now wants to make him pay for it.

Nigel Dewbury – solicitor and leading light of the Stratford Players. Pompous, stuck-up and self-regarding, he believes he is the star of the show, and should play all the leading roles. He also fancies his romantic chances with Dorothy.

Mary Plunkett – owner of the Rectory bed and breakfast. Jolly, generous and an unashamedly adoring Jefferson Steel fan – although somewhat confused about which roles he played in his films, and how keen he is on her.

Denis Dobbins – handyman and village Mr Fixit. Avuncular though slightly dull, Denis is star-struck by Jefferson and fancies heading up his entourage of one.

Lauren Bell – thirty-something marketing executive former physiotherapist and the sponsor's wife. Passionate about the arts and smarter than her husband allows her to be, she's treated as a bimbo because of her looks.

Journalists – we only hear them offstage.

ACT ONE

Scene One

DOROTHY, MARY *and* NIGEL *at a trestle table on the stage of the Barn Theatre.* DOROTHY NETTLE *is an attractive, middle-class English woman in her late thirties who takes little care over her appearance. She is friendly, good natured but nobody's fool.* DOROTHY *is on her feet appearing to address a crucial public meeting.*

DOROTHY Thank you all so much for coming. You are the most important people in any theatre. Without you there is no play. Without you there is no drama. Without you there is only silence. You may think you are sitting in an old barn with uncomfortable seats and inadequate heating. But you are not. You are sitting in the court at Elsinore, you are in the forest of Arden. You are on the steps of the senate in Rome. This humble theatre is a portal, a door to a world of imagination that can transport us from our humdrum existence and allow us to take part in the greatest stories ever told. And this door is about to be closed. The council has withdrawn its grant and unless we can raise fifty thousand pounds it is going to sell the building to be turned into executive homes. I know executives need homes but they also need dreams. Which is why I implore you, I beg you to take this last chance to save our theatre. If not, the community will not just lose its theatre. It will lose its soul.

MARY *and* NIGEL *applaud.*

NIGEL Very eloquent Dorothy. I couldn't have put it better myself – well I could probably, the emotion was perhaps a touch overwrought at the end…

MARY Oh do shut up Nigel. I thought it was bloody marvellous honest Dot I'm welling up here.

DOROTHY But will it work?

MARY Only one way to find out.

NIGEL Let's let the public in. That is the point of a public meeting after all. Denis if you would be so kind as to open the doors.

We hear a **VOICE** *from the back.*

DENIS I have opened the doors.

DENIS *walks down to the front.*

I'm afraid no one's come.

DOROTHY What? No one?

DENIS Well it's a cold night and you're up against Strictly...

Pause as the bad news sinks in.

DOROTHY So that's it then. There is to be no last appeal.

MARY Maybe people felt the last "Last appeal" was one last appeal too many?

DOROTHY They've given up on us.

NIGEL And so the final curtain descends...la commedia e finita...

DENIS Don't be so dramatic, Nigel.

NIGEL I thought that was the whole point?

MARY Maybe we should give it ten minutes.

DOROTHY I have given it ten years, Mary. Not to mention a second mortgage.

NIGEL If you need a shoulder to cry on.

NIGEL *places a consoling arm around* **DOROTHY**'s *shoulders which she deftly removes.*

ACT ONE, SCENE ONE

DOROTHY Thanks Nigel, but perhaps what I really need is to face the truth. ~~Who am I kidding~~? Maybe no one wants to see us prancing about in fancy dress spouting words written hundreds of years ago.

DENIS Shall we all go home then? We could catch the end of Strictly...

MARY If we had a star people would come.

NIGEL Well actually I was described as the star of our Toad of Toad Hall...

MARY A real star Nigel. Someone who has been on telly or in films.

~~**DOROTHY** Mary might have a poin~~t.

NIGEL Is there no escaping celebrity culture?

MARY And if we got a star we could get publicity.

DOROTHY And if we got publicity we could get sponsorship.

DENIS That's sorted then.

MARY So who are we going to get?

NIGEL How about...nobody in their right mind?

pause

journalists in auditorium
Peter up SC steps

LX 4 } cue as Nigel starts to move
FX 4 } airport noises (plays out)

Scene Two

We are at a press conference at Heathrow Airport featuring **JEFFERSON STEEL**. **JEFFERSON** *is an ageing Hollywood star, good looking, charming, arrogant and insecure. He is good at being a celebrity and enjoys the showbiz spotlight. During the conference flash bulbs pop and the* **JOURNALISTS** *shout his name to try and get his attention.*

JEFFERSON It's great to be back. I love this place.

FIRST JOURNALIST *(o.s.)* What, Heathrow?

JEFFERSON And your crazy English sense of humour! You guys slay me.

SECOND JOURNALIST *(o.s.)* Mr. Steel, Mr. Steel – this is a pretty big departure for your career isn't it?

JEFFERSON Not really. I'm an actor. Acting's what I do. Theatre has always been my first love. And deep down I've always wanted to repay my debt to the muse.

FIRST JOURNALIST *(o.s.)* Ever since they cancelled your last movie?

JEFFERSON *(laughs without amusement)* No...the Ultimate Finality franchise had reached the end of its natural life and I had been looking for fresh challenges.

SECOND JOURNALIST *(o.s.)* What made you say "yes" to Shakespeare?

JEFFERSON I get sent hundreds of scripts every week. This one stood out.

THIRD JOURNALIST *(o.s.)* Why?

JEFFERSON The writing. Showed real talent.

FIRST JOURNALIST *(o.s.)* But can an American action hero really *be* King Lear?

ACT ONE, SCENE TWO

JEFFERSON To be, or not to be. That is the question.

JEFFERSON *is pleased with himself despite getting the wrong play.*

Besides, my agent tells me I get all the good lines and I'm in every scene.

FIRST JOURNALIST *(o.s.)* Yeah. But isn't it going to be a bit of a comedown for a star like yourself performing in such a small theatre?

JEFFERSON If there's only one person out there, then I'll play to them. And I follow in illustrious theatrical footsteps. Many fellow Hollywood stars have performed in England. Nicole, Dustin, Gwyneth, Spacey. But none before have performed Shakespeare in... Stratford. This marks the pinnacle of my career. Jefferson Steel is at the top of his game.

SECOND JOURNALIST *(o.s.)* But you'll be acting with amateurs.

JEFFERSON You guys are too hard on yourselves. Some British actors aren't so bad.

THIRD JOURNALIST *(o.s.)* So are you really going to save the theatre?

JEFFERSON *gives them a big Hollywood smile.*

JEFFERSON It's a tall order, but as Jack Finality says to the president at the end of Ultimate Finality Four – I'll give it my best shot.

STEEL *mimes shooting a gun and blowing away the smoke. Press conference footage ends. Darkness.*

Scene Three

Suddenly the door opens, **DOROTHY** *stands at the door, laden with luggage.*

DOROTHY Ladies and gentlemen I give you Mr. Jefferson Steel!

JEFFERSON *enters and the cast of four all stand up and applaud.* **JEFFERSON** *takes stock of the scene and goes into phoney actor mode.*

JEFFERSON Thank you guys. You are too kind.

More applause.

DOROTHY May I say on behalf of us all that it is a privilege and an honour to share a stage with you. You were our first choice and the very top of our wish list.

More applause.

JEFFERSON Thank you. There is nothing more humbling for an actor than to receive the approbation of his peers.

DOROTHY So first, allow me to present our valiant stage management team, who will also be taking some of the smaller roles.

TEAM *(shy, nervous)* Hello!

DOROTHY And may I introduce you to your fellow players? Denis Dobbins who is taking the role of the Earl of Gloucester.

DENIS *is an overweight, middle-aged man wearing overalls.*

DENIS Wotcha.

He does a matey thumbs up. **DOROTHY** *continues the introductions.*

DOROTHY Mary Plunkett who is playing Goneril. And probably Regan. There is a certain amount of doubling up but I think it could be interesting theatrically...

MARY is flushed and curtsies. JEFFERSON is unsure what is going on.

MARY It's an honour Mr. Steel. And can I say that you're so much younger than you look in your films.

JEFFERSON is not amused.

Not that you look old in them. You look young, very young...

Struggling.

...especially the old ones...

JEFFERSON Thank you.

MARY I love all your films. Particularly The Fugitive.

JEFFERSON That wasn't me.

MARY Are you sure?

JEFFERSON Yah, I think I'd remember.

DOROTHY hurries on with introductions.

DOROTHY And of course Nigel Dewbury who will be giving us his Earl of Kent.

NIGEL is the classic am-dram performer, more luvvie than the genuine article. He is middle-aged and wears a smart blazer and bow tie. NIGEL gives an ironic and elaborate Shakespearean bow.

NIGEL The privilege is all mine.

He clearly does not mean this.

DENIS has come round again for another introduction.

DOROTHY ...and this is Denis, again, who is also playing Edgar...

DENIS Yeah, Jeff – I wonder if you would mind being in a selfie?

He holds out mobile phone to take it and is told off by **DOROTHY**.

DOROTHY Denis...

JEFFERSON Whoa, whoa. Excuse me...

Pulls **DOROTHY** *aside.*

...but I've never heard of any of these people...where's Judi Dench, Kenny Branagh, Maggie Smith?

JEFFERSON *looks up to see the cast are listening intently.*

DOROTHY All otherwise engaged I'm afraid!

JEFFERSON We've got a problem here. I need to talk to the director.

DOROTHY You are.

JEFFERSON *You're* the director?

DOROTHY Yes I am.

JEFFERSON I thought you were the driver.

DOROTHY I'm that too.

JEFFERSON *is beginning to panic. What has he let himself in for?*

MARY She's also playing the Fool. She's very good – she used to be in the business...

JEFFERSON What?

DOROTHY But as the *director* I would quite like to have a gentle read-through, just to get an initial feel for the play, OK?

JEFFERSON *is losing it.*

JEFFERSON Jefferson Steel does not do read-throughs. I am not sitting around listening to everyone else's lines. And don't tell me this dump is the rehearsal room!

DOROTHY Oh no.

JEFFERSON Thank God!

DOROTHY *This* is our theatre.

JEFFERSON *(incredulous)* Here?!

DOROTHY Yes.

NIGEL "A poor thing but our own..."

JEFFERSON Jeez! What has the Royal Shakespeare Company come to?

NIGEL The Royal Shakespeare Company?

JEFFERSON My agent said I was playing Lear at Stratford.

DOROTHY And so you are.

NIGEL We are the Stratford Players.

JEFFERSON Stratford, right – where Shakespeare was born?

DOROTHY Er...not exactly. This is Stratford. But it isn't on Avon.

It's Stratford St. John...in Suffolk. We're just a small amateur drama group.

JEFFERSON *realises that the people in front of him are not professional actors at all but local people. He nods calmly taking it all in – and then screams...*

JEFFERSON AAAAARRRRRGHHHH!!!

JEFFERSON *is ballistic, trying to get a response from his cell phone. The cast follow him round the theatre, keen to watch a celebrity in action.*

I am going to kill my agent. Charlie Rosen is a dead man.

DOROTHY I did explain all this in my letter to Mr. Rosen. The council has cut off our funding so unless we raise the money we have to close.

JEFFERSON And when I have killed Charlie Rosen, I am going to dig him up and kill him again...

DOROTHY You see, a big name means big sponsorship and big publicity. You're going to save our little theatre.

JEFFERSON I'm sorry to disappoint you lady, but Jefferson Steel is not so washed up he has to do charity gigs.

MARY But you promised. It was on the news. You were really inspiring.

DENIS "Theatre is in my blood" and all that stuff. Very moving.

JEFFERSON I was *acting* you idiot!

He keeps punching numbers into his cell phone.

(On phone) Charlie Rosen, you moron, you booked me into the wrong goddam Stratford! This is Stratford on Pigshit in Nowheresville...

NIGEL Really!

JEFFERSON *(on phone)* What do you mean you knew? No I won't calm down, I am going to rip out your vital organs and stuff them down your throat...

NIGEL Charming!

JEFFERSON *(on phone)* You've got to get me out of here. Charlie. *Now!*

Pause.

It can't be too late. It was just one lousy press conference. No one saw it.

DENIS Six o'clock news over here.

JEFFERSON *(on phone)* ...and every network in the States...oh great... No Charlie I am NOT PLEASED!

DENIS *is looking at his mobile.*

DENIS Oh look you're trending on Twitter – and the press conference is on YouTube...

JEFFERSON *(to Charlie on mobile)* No, you halfwit I am not making a noble sacrifice and going back to my theatrical roots – I'm stuck in Loserville with a bunch of amateurs. Hello? Hello? Holy crap!

NIGEL I'm afraid we have a "save the theatre" swear box...

He produces swear box.

JEFFERSON I don't give a *fuck*. And I am not saving your *fucking* theatre!

Enter **LAUREN**, *an attractive trophy wife of the brewer sponsor who is not taken seriously because of her looks. She is nervous about the project because the sponsorship was her idea.*

LAUREN Everything all right?

DOROTHY Mr. Steel, may I introduce Lauren Bell who is the public relations director of our sponsor who very kindly paid for your flights and is meeting a lot of the production costs.

LAUREN Mr. Steel I'm a big, big fan of yours.

JEFFERSON *clocks that she is quite good looking.*

JEFFERSON That makes two of us. So who is this sponsor? Global bank? Blue chip multinational?

LAUREN It's Bell Ales – Suffolk's premier independent brewery.

JEFFERSON So we're talking chicken feed.

LAUREN *looks hurt at this rudeness.*

DOROTHY Mr. Steel is a bit upset as there has been something of a misunderstanding. He thought he was playing Lear in Stratford on Avon...

LAUREN Oh dear. That's not going to be a problem is it?

JEFFERSON *is a broken man.*

DENIS No it's an easy mistake to make...there are several Stratfords in Britain. There's Stratford in East London...

NIGEL Stratford Tony in Wiltshire...

DENIS Stratford St. Agnes in Somerset...

DOROTHY OK. I think Mr. Steel gets the picture.

DENIS ...Stratford St. Andrew and Stratford St. Mary, Stratford St. Peter, Stratford St. Bernard...

JEFFERSON Can you do me a favour...?

JEFFERSON *cannot remember* **DENIS***'s name.* **DENIS** *supplies it.*

DENIS Denis.

JEFFERSON Right, Denis. Can you do me a favour Denis...and shut the fuck up?

DOROTHY I think Mr. Steel is probably very tired from his flight. Perhaps he would like to go and have a rest.

JEFFERSON Good idea. Just take me to the hotel.

DOROTHY You're not in a hotel as such Mr. Steel. We are putting you up in Mary's bed and breakfast.

JEFFERSON This cannot be happening to me!

LAUREN We thought you would prefer somewhere unpretentious.

JEFFERSON Well you were wrong! I definitely prefer pretentious.

JEFFERSON *walks out of the door and on the way shouts.*

MARY Mr. Steel you've forgotten your bags.

JEFFERSON *returns.*

JEFFERSON No, *you've* forgotten my bags.

ACT ONE, SCENE THREE

He exits again. **DOROTHY** *and* **MARY** *look at each other and then pick up his bags.*

DOROTHY *sings the* **FOOL***'s song to cover the scene change.*

DOROTHY/FOOL
HE THAT HAS AND A LITTLE TINY WIT -
WITH HEY, HO, THE WIND AND THE RAIN -
MUST MAKE CONTENT WITH HIS FORTUNES FIT,
FOR THE RAIN IT RAINETH EVERY DAY.

puts hat back
LX 7 b&b lights
FX 6 seagulls
table & chair on SR
as she puts hat back

Gin take green jacket to SL

Peter enters FS: once table set

Scene Four

MARY's bed and breakfast. We see a table with a small checkered tablecloth.

JEFFERSON sits at the table, tired and grumpy. MARY flounces in with a marked coquettishness holding notepad.

MARY Good morning Mr. Steel.

Takes pad and pen from her hand as though it is an autograph.

JEFFERSON All right! Just this once. Who shall I make it to?

MARY Actually, I was going to take your order. Not that I am not a big fan which I am. Die Hard was one of my all time favourites.

JEFFERSON That was Bruce Willis. And he is bald.

MARY Well you are just like him – except not bald of course.

JEFFERSON hands back pad.

So. What can I get you?

JEFFERSON How about a room at the Four Seasons?

MARY Would you like a full English breakfast?

JEFFERSON That's a no. I want guava juice, egg-white fritata with brocollini rice cheese and peppers.

A beat as MARY takes in what he is saying.

MARY I've got toast...

JEFFERSON Forget it. Just get me a skinny latte decaf with soya milk and an extra shot...

MARY Nescafe OK?

JEFFERSON I give up. Can you do water? Do you have water here? Has drinking water arrived in England?

MARY One lovely glass of fresh water coming up...

She goes off to the kitchen. **JEFFERSON** *gets out a big box of pills of various colours which he arranges in a line.* **MARY** *reappears with a glass of water.*

Do you feel alright Mr. Steel?

JEFFERSON I will when I've got these inside me...

MARY That's a lot of pills.

JEFFERSON Not compared to what I used to take. Just your regular multi-vits. A few uppers, a few downers to counteract the uppers, more uppers to counteract the downers, omega oil, pro-biotics, anti-oxidants...

MARY What's the little blue one?

JEFFERSON That's Jefferson's bedroom buddy...

MARY *is a bit flustered.* **JEFFERSON** *chugs down all the pills.*

MARY You certainly look after yourself Mr. Steel.

JEFFERSON My body is a temple...

MARY ...though it looks more like a pharmacy...but in a good way.

JEFFERSON Thanks for breakfast I'll go pack my bags.

MARY Why?

JEFFERSON I'm checking out.

MARY Oh...

MARY *looks crestfallen.* **JEFFERSON** *exits.* **DOROTHY** *enters.*

DOROTHY *(to* **MARY***)* So? What's King Lear like this morning? Still grumpy?

MARY He says he wants to check out.

DOROTHY Well he's a real charmer isn't he?

MARY It's how these big stars get into their characters. It's what they call method acting. You see King Lear is really grumpy...

DOROTHY *(sarcastically)* And if he was playing Romeo he'd be a real sweetie.

MARY I'd love to see him playing Romeo. He'd look good in tights...and a codpiece...

DOROTHY Mary...too much detail...

MARY I am just saying that he would be very good as a romantic lead.

DOROTHY He's had enough practise in real life. Apparently he's a sexaholic. I read it in a magazine. He's insatiable. Anything in a skirt.

MARY *smooths down her dress hopefully.*

MARY Really?

JEFFERSON *re-enters.*

JEFFERSON Can you tell the concierge my bags are ready?

DOROTHY Good morning Mr. Steel.

JEFFERSON *You* again?

JEFFERSON *can't remember her name.*

DOROTHY Dorothy.

JEFFERSON Dorothy. I want you to tell your people that I'm not happy with the accommodation.

DOROTHY *turns to* **MARY** *in a very formal way.*

DOROTHY Mary. Apparently Mr. Steel isn't happy with the accommodation.

MARY *is crestfallen.*

ACT ONE, SCENE FOUR 17

MARY *(to* **DOROTHY***)* I'm very sorry. He's in the best room I've got.

DOROTHY *turns back to* **JEFFERSON** *in the same formal way.*

DOROTHY The management is very sorry Mr. Steel but you are occupying the best room available.

JEFFERSON You're kidding, right?

DOROTHY *(to* **MARY***)* Mary. Are you kidding?

DOROTHY *looks at* **MARY***'s face then turns back to* **JEFFERSON***.*

She's not kidding.

JEFFERSON But the room doesn't have an en-suite.

MARY The facilities are only just down the hall.

JEFFERSON I found them. Eventually. Only after stumbling into some broad's room who was snoring like a foghorn...

MARY Yes well I am terribly sorry that room is all I have.

JEFFERSON Come on. Next you'll be telling me you don't have a health club!

DOROTHY Nor does Mary have a banqueting suite or conferencing facilities. The clue is in the words "bed" and "breakfast". I am afraid this job will require you to make a few compromises.

JEFFERSON *is getting increasingly panicky.*

JEFFERSON I am not an unreasonable man. I can do compromise. Ask my ex-wife. She got everything. But as a Hollywood A-lister you must understand that I have to maintain my status.

MARY I can see that, yes.

JEFFERSON Otherwise the rest of the cast won't respect me. It's a natural hierarchy.

So as the guy at the top of the food chain I do have a few very basic requirements.

DOROTHY Of course you do.

DOROTHY *gets out her notebook.*

JEFFERSON I want a minibar, home cinema, pool table, jukebox…

DOROTHY *scribbles.*

DOROTHY Is that all?

JEFFERSON No. I also want fresh flowers daily, oh and a dietician and a personal trainer.

DOROTHY Well that's certainly not unreasonable. We will certainly see what we can do won't we Mary? In the meantime shall I take you to the rehearsal?

MARY I'll catch up with you later.

MARY *clears table.*

JEFFERSON OK – where's the car?

DOROTHY There isn't a car, sorry, and unfortunately the helicopter is out of service so I am afraid we are going to have to walk.

JEFFERSON Nobody walks in L.A.

DOROTHY Oh you'll find its really very easy. You just put one foot in front of the other. You'll soon get the hang of it.

They begin walking away from the bed and breakfast round the back of the set (or across the auditorium).

JEFFERSON Add that to my list. I want a limo to take me to and from the set.

DOROTHY It really isn't very far.

ACT ONE, SCENE FOUR

JEFFERSON I don't care how far it is, it is totally unreasonable to expect your leading actor on top of all his other responsibilities and commitments to have to trek all the way...

DOROTHY We are here.

JEFFERSON Oh.

They are now at the barn/rehearsal room. They enter to find that **DENIS** *is already there.*

DENIS Morning Dorothy. Morning Mr. Steel.

DOROTHY Morning Denis.

DENIS How was your journey?

JEFFERSON Unacceptably long.

DENIS I know what you mean. I got held up on Crackett's Lane, they've got one of them big hedge-cutters and the traffic has backed up beyond the silage depot and you wouldn't believe Mr. Steel...

JEFFERSON Denis. It is Denis isn't it? Can we just get one thing straight here?

DENIS Yeah. Sure.

JEFFERSON Denis – you're mistaking me for someone who gives a shit.

DENIS Fair enough.

DOROTHY *trying to make amends for this rudeness.*

DOROTHY Anyway you are here now Denis which is the main thing. Ready and keen to rehearse. Which is always a bonus when you are putting on a play.

Looks at **JEFFERSON**.

DENIS Now just checking, Dorothy, am I Gloucester today? Or Albany? Or Edgar? I wasn't sure whether to bring the beard.

He has fake beard in his hand.

DOROTHY It's a bit early for costume, Denis. You are Gloucester today.

Enter **NIGEL** *with a flourish.*

NIGEL Enter the Earl of Kent, centre stage.

DOROTHY Hello Nigel. OK. That's all of us I think. Apologies from Rupert who is the Duke of Cornwall amongst others – and from Janice who *would* be playing Cordelia but isn't – so I am.

JEFFERSON This sounds kind of desperate.

DOROTHY No this is actually quite a good turnout. And doubling up is part of the fun.

JEFFERSON Fun?

DOROTHY That's the idea.

Enter **MARY**.

MARY Sorry everyone. Mr. Steel you left your glasses in your room.

JEFFERSON I don't wear glasses.

MARY They were by your bed.

JEFFERSON You must be mistaken. Jefferson Steel has twenty twenty vision.

MARY Of course. And you had infra red eyes in the Terminator... that was a good film...

JEFFERSON That was Schwarzenegger.

DOROTHY *hands* **JEFFERSON** *his script.*

DOROTHY Good well that's cleared that up. So shall we take it from Lear's first big speech. On page five.

ACT ONE, SCENE FOUR

Check have Lauren [handwritten annotation]

JEFFERSON *holds the script a long way away from him and clearly has trouble reading it.*

I think the glasses would be a good prop. Shall we try it with the glasses?

JEFFERSON *puts on half-moon glasses which make him look old.*

JEFFERSON You're the director...unbelievably.

DOROTHY Good...so let's give it a whirl.

JEFFERSON/LEAR *(begins to read grudgingly)* "Give me the map there".

He then stops.

JEFFERSON What map? I haven't got a map. How am I going to do this without a map? First line and the whole thing's fallen apart.

DOROTHY Just pretend for now.

NIGEL It's called acting.

JEFFERSON *looks annoyed.*

JEFFERSON/LEAR Know that we have divided
In three our kingdom; and 'tis our fast intent
To shake all cares and business from our age,
Conferring them on younger strengths, while we
Unburthen'd, crawl towards death.

During this, we see the rest of the company whose deference visibly drains away as the poetry is subsumed by his over-naturalistic delivery. The intonation is all wrong and he seems to want to get through it as quickly as possible.

NIGEL Oh really! This is terrible!

JEFFERSON Hey buddy – I agree – but don't blame me. I didn't write this shit!

DOROTHY Can we please carry on...

JEFFERSON/LEAR Tell me, my daughters –

Since now we will divest us both of rule

Interest of territory, cares of state –

Which of you shall we say doth love us most?

That we our largest bounty may extend

Where nature doth with merit challenge

Gone...goner...

DOROTHY Goneril.

MARY *(brightly)* That's me! She's the one who says she loves you but doesn't really though that's only the character obviously not in real life though that's not to say that I don't like you... but that...um...sorry.

MARY blushes.

JEFFERSON ...and your point is?

DOROTHY *(trying to retrieve the situation)* The point is that Mary's character is pronounced Goneril. You do know the play don't you Mr. Steel?

JEFFERSON Sure. It's about a guy whose daughters drive him nuts.

DOROTHY And you have...read it?

JEFFERSON *(beat)* I prefer to start rehearsals with a blank canvas.

The awful truth has struck DOROTHY.

DOROTHY You haven't read it.

NIGEL He hasn't even read the play.

DOROTHY *(raising voice with barely controlled panic)* Please tell me you've read the play!

Enter **LAUREN**.

LAUREN Everything going OK?

DOROTHY Everything's fine. Going well. We're all learning a lot. Jefferson, you remember Lauren?

JEFFERSON Sure, Lauren...

Pause.

...no.

JEFFERSON *rudely doesn't remember her.*

DOROTHY She handles PR for our sponsor. She's probably the most important person here.

JEFFERSON Wrong again!

DOROTHY Perhaps we should take a break here?

JEFFERSON At last a good idea!

NIGEL We've only been rehearsing for five minutes.

JEFFERSON *takes out a cigar.*

DENIS Oops sorry Jeff but as well as the Duke of Gloucester I am the company health and safety officer and I am afraid you're not allowed to smoke in a public building.

JEFFERSON It's not a public building its barely a barn!

DENIS You don't want to set off the sprinklers.

JEFFERSON *grunts.*

DOROTHY Why don't you go outside, have your cigar, relax and maybe have a look at the play. Apparently it's quite good.

JEFFERSON *looks at her with the beginning of a grudging respect for cheerily standing up to him.*

JEFFERSON You know what happened to the last director who thought they knew better than me?

DOROTHY They won an Oscar?

JEFFERSON *laughs at this rudeness.*

JEFFERSON Funny. I can see why you're playing the Fool.

DOROTHY *points to door.* **JEFFERSON** *exits the barn.*

DOROTHY Back in five minutes?

JEFFERSON Do I have a choice?

DOROTHY *(with inappropriate cheeriness)* That's the spirit.

LAUREN *takes* **DOROTHY** *to one side.*

LAUREN So Mr. Steel *is* happy is he? Only you know what the chairman's like and he wasn't very keen to do this anyway...

DOROTHY Yes we are all indebted to you Lauren, it can't have been easy persuading your husband...

LAUREN Theatre is not really Colin's thing. He is more of a monster truck-racing man...

DOROTHY Well you are making a very noble gesture, patronising the arts.

LAUREN Colin's basically interested in selling beer in the interval.

NIGEL *is reciting verse to* **DENIS** *and* **MARY** *in another grouping.*

NIGEL ...Here I disclaim all my paternal care,

Propinquity and property of blood,

And as a stranger to my heart and me

Hold thee from this for ever...

DENIS Give it a rest Nigel. We know you know all your lines.

MARY They are not his lines. They're Lear's lines.

NIGEL It's not fair. I should be Lear. It's every actor's dream.

DENIS You're a lawyer Nige. Get over it.

NIGEL What has Jefferson Steel got that I haven't?

MARY Mmm...good looks, fame, money...how long have you got?

NIGEL Well thank you for that vote of confidence. But in terms of acting, let's face it he's no Laurence Olivier.

MARY That's unfair. It's early days and we shouldn't make any rash judgements...because I think he is totally fantastic.

The others all look at each other knowingly, amused at her besotted condition. **DOROTHY** *hands her a napkin.*

DOROTHY Mary, you're dribbling.

JEFFERSON *re-enters.*

JEFFERSON Jeez it's cold! A guy could catch his death smoking out there!

He's making a call on his mobile.

Hey Charlie! Have you got me out of it yet? No? Then you're still dead. Oh great! What does Poison Barbie want now? No out of the question. When? OK, but I don't need this Charlie...

Call ends.

DOROTHY Bad news?

JEFFERSON Yeah. I'm still here.

DOROTHY Mr. Rosen thought this would be good for you.

JEFFERSON Charlie Rosen is a lying thieving scumbag son of a bitch.

DOROTHY Particularly since you weren't getting a flood of other offers...

JEFFERSON Things are quiet at the moment. Right across the industry. You ask anyone.

DOROTHY But since things *are* quiet, temporarily, maybe you should make the best of it.

NIGEL That's certainly what the rest of us will have to do.

DOROTHY So homework: by next rehearsal I want everyone to be familiar with the whole text...

Looks at **JEFFERSON**.

...as we haven't got the luxury of much time. So when we come back to Act One perhaps you could all have had a think about your motivation.

JEFFERSON My motivation is that I'll look like a complete schmuck if I don't stick with this lousy job.

LAUREN *hears this and looks worried.*

DOROTHY He's just joking Lauren. Theatrical badinage.

JEFFERSON The beer broad. You still here?

LAUREN If you don't mind I've brought you some samples of our product to try.

JEFFERSON What samples?

LAUREN *produces bottles.*

LAUREN Well there's Harvest Gold, Nutty Badger and – and this one, which we've named to tie in with the show.

JEFFERSON Tell me the worst.

LAUREN "King Beer". You see like "King Lear", only...

JEFFERSON That's terrible.

DENIS *is looking at the label.*

DENIS True – but I reckon it will do the job. Couple of pints of this and even Nigel will look attractive.

ACT ONE, SCENE FOUR 27

LAUREN Go on Mr. Steel – try it. Can I get a picture of you drinking it for our website?

She opens bottle, hands it to JEFFERSON, *and hands camera to* DENIS. *They pose.* JEFFERSON *reluctantly takes a swig – and spits it out.*

JEFFERSON Jeez! *spits beer cue LX11 centre spot — Bucket & Mop SL*

DOROTHY *(weakly to* LAUREN*)* Sorry. Jet lag.

We hear another FOOL*'s song, sung by* DENIS *as he mops up.*

DENIS/FOOL
THEN THEY FOR SUDDEN JOY DID WEEP,
AND I FOR SORROW SUNG,
THAT SUCH A KING SHOULD PLAY BO-PEEP AND GO THE
    FOOLS AMONG.

puts hat on stand cue LX12
transition into barn
FX7 seagulls over change

Scene Five

Barn before the next rehearsal. Bits of set are beginning to be assembled. **DOROTHY** *is hammering angrily.* **JEFFERSON** *is reading* **LEAR** *half-heartedly.*

JEFFERSON What's your problem? Why are you still so angry?

DOROTHY All you had to do was drink the beer!

JEFFERSON It was disgusting. I've tasted better spinal fluid. Don't ask.

DOROTHY She was trying to be friendly

JEFFERSON By poisoning me? She's a madwoman.

DOROTHY She's backing this production.

JEFFERSON Point proven.

DOROTHY Tell me – do you deliberately set out to offend people?

JEFFERSON Nope. It just comes naturally.

DOROTHY Luckily I think I managed to cover up for you.

JEFFERSON The jet lag happens to be true. I couldn't sleep last night – well not till I started reading the play.

DOROTHY So you *still* haven't read it?

JEFFERSON Yes I have and I found it incredibly...

DOROTHY Yes?

JEFFERSON ...*long*.

DOROTHY Anything else?

JEFFERSON I have some issues.

DOROTHY Issues?

    JEFFERSON *gets out his copy of the play.*

JEFFERSON To be honest I think it needs a rewrite.

DOROTHY But this is Shakespeare!

JEFFERSON Nobody's perfect. The five-act structure doesn't work. It's way too wordy. I say we cut two acts and give it a happy ending.

DOROTHY *(amused)* We are doing the play as written.

JEFFERSON Have you never heard of improvisation? Where I come from the script is a springboard for the actor to bounce off.

DOROTHY You can't improvise Shakespeare. How would you do the scene on the heath?

JEFFERSON We're not doing the scene on the heath.

DOROTHY It's the most famous speech in the play, possibly in all Shakespeare's works! "Blow, winds, and crack your cheeks! Rage! Blow! You cataracts and hurricanoes, spout; Till you have drench'd our steeples, drown'd the cocks!"

JEFFERSON I can do it with a look.

DOROTHY It's essential to the play!

JEFFERSON Jefferson Steel doesn't do crazy. All that looney-toons stuff has gotta go.

DOROTHY *(smiling at him)* Do I detect a hint of panic? All those words? All that acting?

JEFFERSON Panic? Jefferson Steel? I just want to get on with the play. Anyway, where is everybody? Why aren't we rehearsing?

DOROTHY It's a weekday. Everyone's got proper jobs. I mean real jobs. I mean...

She is digging herself into a hole and gives up.

...they will be here shortly...

JEFFERSON So what am I going to do in the meantime?

I can't hang out in my trailer...because I don't have a trailer.

DOROTHY You could always learn those lines.

JEFFERSON Nyeh! I'm going to take a tour of downtown.

JEFFERSON *leaves the rehearsal room.* **DOROTHY** *starts getting out the tools including hammer and nail gun for making scenery and begins work on a flat.* **NIGEL** *enters.*

NIGEL Dorothy – may I have a word?

DOROTHY What is it?

NIGEL I have an announcement to make. I am leaving the Stratford Players.

DOROTHY Oh not again!

NIGEL I am sorry but it is a matter of principle.

DOROTHY The principle being that you didn't get the best part. Don't be so pompous.

NIGEL I am not being pompous. That appalling American is a disgrace to the traditions of the amateur stage and the noble name of the Stratford Players.

DOROTHY That sounds pompous to me.

NIGEL For you, Dorothy, I was prepared to humiliate myself and play the Earl of Kent.

DOROTHY It is a very difficult part Nigel, and you're the only one who can do it.

NIGEL You really think so?

DOROTHY Remember the judge at that drama festival in Norwich?

NIGEL *(fake modesty)* Oh, I'm not sure, it was all a long time ago.

DOROTHY One of the best Malvolios he had seen...

NIGEL *(interrupts)* "*The* best Malvolio ever seen in the history of the East Anglia Drama Festival", were... I think...his exact words.

DOROTHY That's why we need you. Anyone can play Lear. Jefferson's just a famous face to raise the money... But how many people can dazzle as Kent. I can think of only one.

NIGEL You're not just saying that to get round me?

DOROTHY takes his hand and looks into his eyes.

DOROTHY *(innocently)* Would I?

Yes she would.

NIGEL "The Gods reward your kindness".

NIGEL leans forward for a kiss. DOROTHY avoids him tactfully. He looks disappointed. She then drops his hand. JEFFERSON returns.

JEFFERSON OK. Taken a tour of downtown. Killed three minutes. Hey Nige. I hope I'm not interrupting anything?

NIGEL Not at all. Just here early for the rehearsal.

DOROTHY Nigel is very keen.

JEFFERSON There's keen and there's desperate...

DOROTHY If you want to be useful perhaps you two could give me a hand...

JEFFERSON Hey, do I look like a carpenter?

He has got the celebrity outfit of sunglasses and baseball hat on.

NIGEL No not really.

NIGEL picks up saw.

JEFFERSON *(to NIGEL)* Are you saying I can't do carpenter? That I wouldn't be convincing as a carpenter? Jesus! Come to think of it I even played Jesus in a biopic. Give me that nail gun.

Enter MARY.

MARY Oooh – you look just like you did in that Bond film.

JEFFERSON That was Connery.

MARY No – he's much younger. Or he was then. Not now, obviously.

Enter **DENIS**.

DENIS Evening! Nice gun. Bosch GSK sixty-four pneumatic brad head. Sweet. And they sorted the jamming problem with the GSK fifty. You can do up to sixty nails a minute…

JEFFERSON *puts nail gun to* **DENIS**'s *head.*

JEFFERSON Feeling lucky, Denis?

MARY Yes! That's the one you were in! You were brilliant in that!

JEFFERSON I *wasn't*! That was *Eastwood*!

JEFFERSON *puts gun to own head.*

DENIS As health and safety officer I'm going to have to insist you put that nail gun down…

JEFFERSON Relax Denis – the safety catch is on.

He pretends to shoot in the air to demonstrate, suddenly nail gun goes off with a bang. **JEFFERSON** *drops it.*

Holy shit!

NIGEL Fellow thespians – and of course Mr. Steel, do you think that now we are all here we might commence the actual rehearsal?

DOROTHY *tidies away set-making equipment.*

DOROTHY Thank you Nigel.

DENIS Ah, Dorothy, would now be a good time to talk about the scene where Gloucester has his eyes put out? I had this idea.

DOROTHY Yes?

ACT ONE, SCENE FIVE

DENIS AS CORNWALL Out, vile jelly! Where is thy lustre now?

DENIS pretends to put out his own eyes, turning away but then turns back round with eyes closed and a ping pong ball in each hand.

DENIS Aargh!!! Whoops!

One of the balls falls to the floor and bounces off.

Pause.

What do you think?

DOROTHY I think it may need a bit of work...

DENIS Leave it with me...

DOROTHY So can we go from Act One Scene Three...places please. Apologies from the Duke of Cornwall – his train's stuck outside Royston and the Duke of Albany's got childcare problems – but he can join us now thanks to the miracle of Skype!

She produces a tablet and places it on a chair. We see **ALBANY**'s *head on it. The tablet is held away from the audience for the dialogue so we just hear the voice over.*

Hello David!

ALBANY ON SKYPE *(voiceover)* Hello Dorothy! Hello Jefferson! Hello Mary!

Downbeat.

Hello Nigel.

DOROTHY Thanks David. I think we'll move you downstage a bit.

The tablet and chair is moved to one side. We now see **ALBANY**'s *disembodied head on the tablet as an interested, but not active participant in the rest of the scene.*

Denis if you could fill in, as and when...

JEFFERSON *sits on a large battered throne and continues his speech.* **NIGEL** *stands beside him, looking decidedly unhappy, and* **DOROTHY** *hovers around with her text.*

JEFFERSON/LEAR Cornwall and Albany...

JEFFERSON *nods to* **ALBANY** *on the tablet screen.*

With my two daughters' dowers digest the third:

I do invest you jointly with my power...

JEFFERSON*'s performance has improved, but is naturalistic – and in stark contrast to* **NIGEL***'s more classic, if overblown, approach.*

Ourself by monthly course,

With reservation of an hundred knights

By you to be sustained, shall our abode

Make with you by due turn;

Only we shall retain

The name and all th'addition to a king.

NIGEL *gives forth: booming, impassioned but very stilted. He stands directly in front of* **JEFFERSON**, *obscuring him.*

NIGEL/KENT Royal Lear,

Whom I have ever honour'd as my King,

Loved as my father, as my master followed,

As my great patron thought on in my prayers, –

JEFFERSON *looks at* **DOROTHY** *in exasperation.*

JEFFERSON This isn't acting for God's sake. It's melodrama. Real people just don't talk like that.

NIGEL I'm playing it in the manner the Bard intended, in the way his plays have been performed through the ages by our great men of the theatre – Olivier, Gielgud, Richardson.

JEFFERSON Try playing it like someone who's still alive.

ACT ONE, SCENE FIVE

DOROTHY I'll do the directing, thank you both. And Albany...

Referring to the tablet.

I think we need you more upstage...

DOROTHY *picks up the tablet, now holding the screen away from the audience.*

ALBANY *(voiceover)* Actually Dorothy, all this noise is waking up the kids...mind if I log off?

DOROTHY No, you do that. No problem. Night!

All cast wave at the screen.

ALL Night David!

DOROTHY *puts tablet aside.*

DOROTHY Now where were we? Yes, Nigel – remember, Kent is Lear's friend. Make him a bit warmer. And Jefferson, I think Lear needs a bit more passion.

NIGEL If only. He's reading it like a bloody shopping list.

JEFFERSON *is annoyed.*

JEFFERSON Hey Nige. How many movies have you made? Not many. Name over the title? Not yours. Sex scenes with Sharon Stone? I don't think so.

MARY He has got a point. And they were excellent sex scenes. So I've heard.

NIGEL The Suffolk Herald said that my Polonius was definitive.

JEFFERSON I rest my case.

The cast snigger at this put down.

NIGEL I defer to the director.

This puts **DOROTHY** *in a difficult position and she tries to compromise diplomatically.*

DOROTHY I think...there is a definitive performance lying somewhere between Californian Realism and English Mellifluence.

JEFFERSON *(angrily)* That's just bullshit... Bullshit! Bullshit! Bullshit! Bullshit! Bullshit!!!

The door opens and there is a girl with suitcases.

JESSICA Dad?

JEFFERSON My God! Jessica! How...

It is his daughter **JESSICA**. **JESSICA** *is seventeen, and smarter than her father. She is also very used to being let down by the dad she once idolised.*

JESSICA You were going to meet me at the airport?

JEFFERSON Was I?

NIGEL *(s.v.)* Oh dear. It's not just his lines he has problems remembering.

JEFFERSON Jessica, cupcake!

JESSICA Please don't call me that.

JEFFERSON This is my daughter.

JEFFERSON *tries to introduce them.*

Jessica, this is...er... Denis.

DOROTHY Dorothy...

NIGEL Nigel.

MARY Mary.

JESSICA Hi.

DOROTHY Jessica – lovely to meet you. Your father's...told us... er...*so* much about you...

JESSICA I doubt it. Unless he's looked me up on Wikipedia.

JEFFERSON Don't be like that.

Awkward silence.

I said I'd look after Jessica for a while. My ex-wife's getting married again.

DOROTHY That's nice.

JEFFERSON Not for the guy who is marrying her!

Nobody laughs.

It's just for the duration of the honeymoon. Which starts...

Checks watch.

JESSICA ...yesterday.

DOROTHY So all quite sudden.

JEFFERSON You wait for the divorce!

Still nobody laughs.

JESSICA It's not funny Dad. You promised you would be there and you weren't.

JEFFERSON Your mom must have told me the wrong landing time. Deliberately, of course – to make me look bad.

JESSICA You don't need any help with that Dad.

DOROTHY Well Jessica – you're very welcome here.

Beat.

Do you want to be in a play?

JEFFERSON *(very forcefully)* No she doesn't!

JESSICA I can answer for myself.

JEFFERSON Non-negotiable. No play. No acting.

JESSICA But...

MARY *leaps in to calm things down.*

MARY We're all so thrilled to have your father here, playing King Lear.

NIGEL (*drily*) Yes indeed! Do you know the piece at all?

JESSICA We did it in high school, remember Dad?

JEFFERSON No.

JESSICA That's cos you weren't there.

To **NIGEL**.

Anyway, he is perfect casting.

JEFFERSON Really?

JESSICA Lear is an arrogant egomaniac and a lousy father all rolled into one.

More awkward silence. **DOROTHY** *fills the gap.*

DOROTHY Well you must be tired – let's get you sorted out with a room.

JEFFERSON I'll help you with your bags.

JESSICA When – tomorrow?

> **JEFFERSON**, **MARY** *and* **JESSICA** *exit. More awkward silence as they all look at each other.*

NIGEL (*very jolly*) At last! Some drama!

We hear the **FOOL**'s *song sung by* **DOROTHY**.

DOROTHY/FOOL
> FATHERS THAT WEAR RAGS SHALL MAKE THEIR CHILDREN BLIND/BUT FATHERS THAT BEAR BAGS SHALL SEE THEIR CHILDREN KIND.

Scene Six

In the bed and breakfast.

JEFFERSON *and* **JESSICA**.

JEFFERSON So long as you're here, you might as well make yourself useful. Test me on my lines. Act Four Scene Six.

JESSICA Do I have a choice?

JEFFERSON That's the spirit!

He tosses her the text. There is a pause. A long pause.

JESSICA "When".

JEFFERSON Sure, I knew that. "When...

JESSICA "When we".

JEFFERSON "When we...er...were..."

JESSICA "Are..."

JEFFERSON "When we are..."

JESSICA "born".

JEFFERSON That's it... "When we are born..."

JESSICA This is hopeless Dad.

She puts down book, recites the speech perfectly.

When we are born, we cry that we are come To this great stage of fools...

She takes a puff from her inhaler.

JEFFERSON You still taking that stuff?

JESSICA Like you're interested.

JEFFERSON I'm your father. Of course I'm interested.

Pause.

What's wrong with you again?

JESSICA I suffer from asthma and I am allergic to a number of things including my father...

JEFFERSON Yeah, yeah I remember. I remember the medical bills anyway. Well kid, we've all got our problems. And mine is that I have more lines in this goddam play than in my last twenty movies combined.

***JEFFERSON** holds up the text in which he has been marking up his lines with a yellow magic marker. He's trying to break the ice a bit.*

I'm scared Jessica.

JESSICA You don't sound it.

JEFFERSON Are you saying I can't do scared? Jefferson Steel can do scared.

JESSICA Yeah, all right Dad, I believe you.

JEFFERSON Now give me a break and show your father a little respect.

*He carries on marking the text with the pen as **JESSICA** effortlessly recites some lines from the play.*

JESSICA AS CORDELIA Good my lord, You have begot me, bred me, loved me: I return those duties back as are right fit, Obey you, love you, and most honour you.

She bows ironically to him after these inappropriate lines.

JEFFERSON That's more like it. But don't get any ideas. You are not going to be in the play.

JESSICA Why not?

JEFFERSON Because...

JESSICA Because I might show you up? I might embarrass you...by being good?

JEFFERSON Because I don't want this for you. You can do better. Become a brain surgeon – or a plumber. Do something more worthwhile than being...an actor.

JESSICA Not all acting has to involve explosions. Some of it can be about truth and emotion.

JEFFERSON Trust me, this business sucks. There are bad people out there – people who will exploit and humiliate a beautiful young girl like you. I know. I'm one of them.

JESSICA Well Dorothy doesn't seem to be a bad person.

JEFFERSON She's an amateur.

JESSICA She's sweet.

JEFFERSON No. She's very cold and uptight and English...

JESSICA Maybe she just doesn't like you.

JEFFERSON What's not to like? Everybody likes Jefferson Steel. It's in the contract.

JESSICA They didn't like you on the plane coming over. The movie was Ultimate Finality.

Pause.

JEFFERSON Which one?

JESSICA Ultimate Finality Three. It was sick.

JEFFERSON That's...good isn't it?

JESSICA Sick as in gross. The girl you kissed at the end could have been your granddaughter. People were booing. With headphones on. The guy next to me said you should be arrested.

JEFFERSON OK. I admit it, I admit it...it's the worst film I've ever been in.

JESSICA That's not true Dad.

JEFFERSON Thank you.

JESSICA It's not as bad as Ultimate Finality Four.

Pause.

JEFFERSON So the therapy going well then?

JESSICA I'm not in therapy.

JEFFERSON Really? Is that normal for a girl your age?

JESSICA You just don't care do you?

JEFFERSON That's unfair. Who bought you a car for your birthday?

JESSICA It was the wrong birthday. You are not allowed to drive at thirteen.

JEFFERSON Who always took you to Disneyland at Christmas?

JESSICA Your agent.

JEFFERSON But I paid for it!

JESSICA You just don't get it, do you Dad?

JEFFERSON I don't get...what?

JESSICA sighs.

I don't need this – and the goddam pen's run out, I've got so many lines!

He throws the marker away. He looks at watch.

I've got to go and rehearse.

He moves off. **JESSICA** *follows.*

Where d'you think you're going?

JESSICA Dorothy said I could help backstage.

JEFFERSON Did she? And what if the star objects?

JESSICA Then the star's daughter will tell her mom about the star's secret bank account that he didn't declare during the divorce proceedings...

ACT ONE, SCENE SIX 43

JEFFERSON You are cruel and heartless.

JESSICA I am my father's daughter...

They walk across stage into rehearsal area where
DOROTHY *is sorting out costumes from pile of jumble.*
DENIS *is fiddling with lights up a ladder.*

DENIS Wotcha Jeff.

JEFFERSON Wotcha... Den.

DOROTHY Good morning your Highness.

JEFFERSON Morning Fool.

DOROTHY You're early. Are you feeling OK?

JEFFERSON It's called being professional.

DOROTHY Of course. Hi Jessica – can you help me with the costumes?

JEFFERSON I don't think so.

JESSICA Love to.

DOROTHY holds up a pair of curtains.

DOROTHY What do you reckon? The Duke of Gloucester's ceremonial robes?

JESSICA Sure.

JEFFERSON Since nobody seems to give a damn whether I am here or not I might as well go have myself a smoke.

DENIS Umbrella?

JEFFERSON Now here's a man who knows how to treat the talent.

DENIS You know that problem you mentioned – I think I've got a solution...

They move outside the barn, to one side of the stage, talking conspiratorially. Meanwhile back in the barn
JESSICA *pulls out a ski hat with bobbles on.*

JESSICA The Fool's cap?

JESSICA puts it on.

(*As* **FOOL**) Nuncle Lear, nuncle Lear, tarry! Take the fool with thee.

DOROTHY You're pretty good. Would it help if I had a word?

JESSICA You think he takes advice? Have you seen his films recently? His clothes? His hair?

DOROTHY You know you are quite hard on him. His heart's in the right place.

JESSICA Unlike his ears.

DOROTHY (*horrified and amused*) No!

JESSICA pulls her face up to her ears to indicate that JEFFERSON has had a face lift.

JESSICA Next time you get close have a look.

DOROTHY I don't intend to get that close.

JESSICA Really? I've heard that before. Still, you're nicer than most of them. And older...

DOROTHY Thank you Jessica – I think. But really I can assure you that your father and I are just – and I mean *only* just – good friends.

JESSICA I'd keep it that way. He's far too in love with himself to be able to love someone else.

DOROTHY It's not all his fault. If you're treated like a king, you're going to end up behaving like one.

JESSICA Oh no – he's getting to you.

JEFFERSON and DENIS re-enter. JEFFERSON has put on baseball cap and dark glasses as befits a celeb – even though it's clearly raining – the umbrella's up.

ACT ONE, SCENE SIX

DENIS So would it be fair to say that I'm, like, your – you know – entourage?

JEFFERSON Sure Den. Maybe entourages are technically more for fixing up drugs and arranging girls than mending plumbing and creosoting fences – but what the hell, buddy, go for it.

DENIS Thanks. So as your entourage, do I keep fans away from you, or encourage them to mob you?

JEFFERSON You keep them away, obviously.

DENIS That's what I don't understand. You want to be so famous that everyone recognises you, but then you put on a baseball cap and dark glasses so nobody does. What's that all about?

JEFFERSON Celebrity's kind of complicated. OK, let's go do this goddam rehearsal.

They re-join the rehearsal. He removes dark glasses and can now see.

I'm back.

DOROTHY Good.

She and **JESSICA** *hold up material across him – as if a cloak.*

Can we just see how this looks?

DENIS Can you keep away from Mr. Steel please...

JEFFERSON It's all right Denis. They're with me.

NIGEL *enters with* **MARY**.

DENIS What about these two?

JEFFERSON I appreciate it Denis – but we'll assume the cast are security cleared.

DENIS *gives him a high five.*

NIGEL *(to* **MARY**) Oh dear. We seem to be witnessing what I think is called a "bromance". I fear I may be sick.

MARY *(worried)* Oh no he's not like *that* at all. We've been getting on so well...

DOROTHY Good evening Nigel, Mary, everyone. Now before we start we have a little surprise for Jefferson.

He asked for a number of riders to his contract – and it's taken a bit of time but I'm delighted to say we can meet his set of minimum requirements.

JESSICA Dad! Are you being ridiculous again?

DOROTHY No, your father's quite right – we have to accept the star needs some basic comforts in order to create an artistic performance worthy of his talents.

JEFFERSON That's more like it. Some free stuff!

DOROTHY *(reads from list)* I have now procured for you your very own personalised executive limo to transport you to and from the theatre.

JEFFERSON About time!

DOROTHY *(calls off)* Denis!

DENIS *enters on what is clearly an old person's mobility buggy.*

DENIS It was my mother's but then the social services said that now that her hip was better she didn't need...sorry, too much information.

DOROTHY We also have your mini-bar.

DENIS *pulls out Tesco bag from shopping basket full of bottles.*

Home cinema and juke box.

DENIS *produces laptop and gives it to* **JEFFERSON**.

Not forgetting your pool table.

DOROTHY *produces the miniature pool sets you buy in the supermarket.*

And of course fresh flowers.

DENIS *produces cheap cellophane wrapped flowers clearly from the garage.* **JEFFERSON** *is despite himself touched by the effort.*

JEFFERSON Not bad. But what about the dietician and personal trainer?

DOROTHY You're looking at her.

DOROTHY *addresses* **JEFFERSON** *as though she were instructor.*

Eat less and walk more, fatty.

JEFFERSON *laughs.*

JEFFERSON *(laughs)* Alright – you win. I'm touched. Jefferson Steel is now officially one hundred percent on board this project!

Some members of the cast cheer.

DOROTHY Thank you! You won't regret it.

JEFFERSON *You* might.

DOROTHY So onwards and upwards – can we go to the scene where Kent and Lear are arguing about the banishment of Cordelia. Jessica – will you be prompt?

JESSICA *(enthusiastically)* Sure!

DOROTHY It's page thirty-two – but you won't be needed because everyone has, I'm sure, learned their lines.

JEFFERSON *begins performing – well – in the scene where* **LEAR** *and* **KENT** *are arguing.* **DENIS** *stands in front of* **JEFFERSON** *facing the audience.*

KENT/NIGEL I'll tell thee thou dost evil.

JEFFERSON/LEAR Hear me recreant. On Thine allegiance hear me. Since thou hast sought to... Since thou hast sought to...

There is a silence which ruins the effect as **JEFFERSON** *has clearly dried. He is prompted by* **JESSICA**.

JESSICA *(whispers)* ...sought to make us break our vow.

JEFFERSON/LEAR ...sought to make us break our vow.

NIGEL *interrupts*.

NIGEL Is this going to happen on the opening night? Will the audience be treated to all of Lear's lines...twice?

JEFFERSON *(bridling)* Hey, some of us have got a lot of lines... and they won't all fit on Denis's back.

DENIS *turns round to reveal a huge cue card attached to his back with the speech on it.*

DOROTHY Denis!

NIGEL I'm sorry Dorothy, the rest of us have gone to a lot of trouble to learn our parts and this is well...it's just very unprofessional.

DOROTHY That's not fair, Nigel. I think we're making good progress.

MARY *(rising up)* And even if Mr. Steel did forget his lines, he forgot them...

Searching for a positive.

...very convincingly.

DOROTHY Are you alright Mary? You've gone bright red.

MARY *fans herself with her script.*

MARY It's very hot in here...

DENIS Plan B Jefferson?

ACT ONE, SCENE SIX

JEFFERSON *gives him the thumbs up.* **DENIS** *goes offstage.*
JEFFERSON *fiddles with his ear.*

DOROTHY Let's take it again from where we stopped. Jefferson if you would be so kind.

JEFFERSON's delivery is rather odd...

JEFFERSON/LEAR Since thou hast sought to make us break our vow which we durst never yet and with strained pride...

Pause.

...pick up from Luton airport to go to Ipswich town centre that's a roger...

[FX 12 feedback noise]

NIGEL My God! He's listening to an earpiece!

DENIS *emerges from wings with script and handset.*

DENIS Sorry Jefferson we're getting some interference...

NIGEL takes the handset from DENIS and shouts into it.

NIGEL What bit of "learn the lines" can't you remember?

JEFFERSON *angrily rips earpiece out.*

JEFFERSON All right all right no need to shout! I'm trying to do my best here for God's sake – saving your asses and what am I getting in return? Nothing!

JESSICA Nothing will come of nothing.

JEFFERSON Shut up you! All I'm asking for is a little respect!

NIGEL You'll find over here that respect has to be earned.

DOROTHY Come on Nigel, you're being unreasonable.

NIGEL *(preening)* Well I expected rather more support than that Dorothy. I have a certain reputation and I won't be treated like this.

JEFFERSON Listen pal you're being an asshole. And if anyone is going to be an asshole round here it's going to be me.

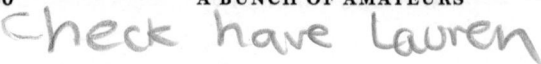

JESSICA That's for sure!

NIGEL It's pronounced "arsehole" actually – and I think you'll find that I am the biggest arsehole here.

DENIS He's not wrong Jefferson.

DOROTHY Please, you two if you do not stop this childish behaviour at once then...

JEFFERSON Then what?

DOROTHY Then I will have no option but to...cry.

Shocked silence. English reserve being tested.

NIGEL Dorothy please don't, I'll stay.

JEFFERSON Let her cry! I've had better directors than Dorothy in tears. Scorsese weeping like a baby. Spielberg sobbing his eyes out.

JESSICA That was when the film came out.

JEFFERSON Not funny!

DOROTHY It was quite funny actually...

NIGEL Hilarious, I thought. And the girl's got good timing – unlike some people.

JEFFERSON *has had enough.*

JEFFERSON I will not be laughed at. Jefferson Steel is not a joke. You asked me to come here.

NIGEL She asked everyone in Hollywood to come here. You were the only one who replied.

DOROTHY Shut up Nigel for God's sake.

JEFFERSON That's it! I don't have to take this shit. I don't have to take any shit. I am Jefferson goddam Steel and I didn't come all the way to Stratford St. Shithole in the United Kingdom of Nowhere to get treated like shit.

DENIS *waves the swear box at him. He is ignored.*

ACT ONE, SCENE SIX 51

Because Jefferson Steel is a four letter word beginning with "S" you probably don't like very much – S – T – A – R. And your *star* has had it with all this charming little English strawberries and cream hogwash! You don't deserve Jefferson Steel. So you can stuff your stupid village, you can stuff your stupid theatre and you can stuff your stupid, knuckle-head, lame-brain retard Shakespeare!

DOROTHY *stands back to admire this rant.*

DOROTHY At last! A full-scale celebrity tantrum! An ego meltdown! I've been waiting for this!

JEFFERSON *is taken aback.* **DOROTHY** *is constantly wrong-footing him.*

JEFFERSON Well, I'm glad to oblige! But no more favours. I'm done here. We're finished! *I quit!*

He exits noisily slamming the door. Enter **LAUREN**.

LAUREN So, everything going well?

Pause and then blackout.

Interval

ACT TWO

Scene One

We are at another rehearsal with **DOROTHY**, **NIGEL**, **MARY**, **JESSICA** *and* **DENIS**.

DOROTHY Good you're here. Jefferson has very kindly agreed to come back in this morning. He was understandably very upset, but I think I may have persuaded him to give us a second chance.

MARY Jefferson's coming.

JEFFERSON *enters angrily.*

DOROTHY Before we start, Nigel's got something to say to Jefferson. Haven't you Nigel?

~~**NIGEL** I think it was Winston Churchill who said we are two nations separated by a common language...~~

~~**DOROTHY** Just get on with the apology Nigel!~~

NIGEL If there has been some misunderstanding, not of my intention, then of course I am sorry. Mea culpa.

NIGEL *performs a theatrical bow.*

JEFFERSON Apology accepted, however over-the-top and unconvincing.

NIGEL *bristles.*

JESSICA Very gracious Dad!

DOROTHY Good, so that's sorted then.

It isn't.

Thank you everyone, places please. Act Five Scene Three. Now the Duke of Cornwall couldn't make it because he's in Cornwall, ironically – and the Duke of Albany has fallen off a castle...

MARY Oh dear!

DOROTHY A bouncy castle...he's twisted his ankle.

DENIS Would this be a good time to discuss my idea for the scene where Gloucester has his eyes put out?

DOROTHY Er... OK?

DENIS/CORNWALL Out, vile jelly! Where is thy lustre now?

DENIS pretends to put out his own eyes, turning away but then turns back round with a fork seemingly in his eye which he pops out. On the end is a pickled onion.

DENIS What do you think?

DOROTHY I think perhaps such magical special effects might detract from the text...

DENIS You're the director.

DENIS shrugs and pops the onion into his mouth.

DOROTHY Now, Jessica if you could resume your vital role as prompt.

JEFFERSON Does she have to?

DOROTHY Yes. And besides it's good for us to have an audience. As a famous American actor once said "If there's only one person out there, then I'll play to them."

JEFFERSON looks suitably embarrassed.

So let's have a bash at the death of Cordelia. Jefferson, if you'd be so kind – it's page fifty-seven.

JEFFERSON I think I know the words to this one.

NIGEL Excellent. Let's see if you can put them in the right order.

DOROTHY Jefferson, this is the climax of your emotional journey. Your favourite daughter is dead – and it's your fault.

JESSICA *(aside)* You don't say!

DOROTHY I want to see love, pain, guilt and anguish.

JEFFERSON Anything else? No? OK.

He gathers himself.

JEFFERSON/LEAR O, you are men of stones:
Had I your tongues and eyes, I'd use them so
That heaven's vault should crack.
She's gone for ever!
I know when one is dead, and when one lives;
She's dead as earth.

We see the emotion in his face. It's a poignant moment.
MARY *applauds excitedly.*

DOROTHY Hands cold Mary?

JESSICA Dad...

JEFFERSON Where did I go wrong?

JESSICA You didn't... I'm just...impressed.

JEFFERSON I'm impressed that you're impressed.

NIGEL Though technically it says Lear should be carrying Cordelia.

JEFFERSON Seriously?

~~**DOROTHY** I was going to come on to that.~~

~~**NIGEL** It shouldn't be hard. Big macho man like you.~~

~~**DENIS** I saw you lift up a tank in Ultimate Finality 2.~~

NIGEL It is the defining image of Lear, carrying his dead daughter...

ACT TWO, SCENE ONE 55

JEFFERSON Sure – I knew that. OK, let's give it a go.

He attempts a fireman's lift.

DOROTHY NOT a fireman's lift!

JEFFERSON *gives it another go, picking her up properly in his arms.*

JEFFERSON *(struggling)* Howl, howl, howl, howl! O, you are men of stones: Jeez! How did Cordelia get so heavy? She should've stuck to skinny lattes...

DOROTHY The text Jefferson, the text.

JEFFERSON No, I'm ok. I'm fine. Howl... Aaaaargh!

DOROTHY That's better...good anguish.

JEFFERSON It's *not* anguish – it's my back!

JEFFERSON uncermoniously drops DOROTHY and staggers off. We hear the FOOL's song.

MARY/FOOL as Dorothy gets hat LX21

THE SWEET AND BITTER FOOL WILL PRESENTLY APPEAR/ THE ONE IN MOTLEY HERE, THE OTHER FOUND OUT THERE

as putting hat back LX22
During speech: Y move bales

grab from inside, bottom
~~right~~ left hand   handle

Scene Two

JEFFERSON *is in his bedroom lying on his front. On top of him, massaging his back is* **LAUREN** *now wearing a tracksuit...*

JEFFERSON Aaargh! Are you sure you know what you are doing?

LAUREN Yes. I am a trained physiotherapist. Before I met Colin this is what I did. I've got a certificate if you don't believe me.

She kneads his back.

JEFFERSON Aaargh! I believe you I believe you!

LAUREN And since we are sponsoring the show I thought I had better help get you back on your feet...

JEFFERSON Aaargh...

LAUREN We've got to loosen up your glutes, its having a knock-on effect and weakening the sacro-iliac.

JEFFERSON You're the back expert.

She manipulates his back again.

LAUREN Yes I am actually. Although Colin seemed to think this was a job for a bimbo...

JEFFERSON Hey Lauren – you're nobody's bimbo. Trust me. I am the bimbo expert. Ow! Are you sure that's helping?

LAUREN Yes. I was really good at this but...

JEFFERSON You realised you didn't have the stomach for torture?

LAUREN No – I met Colin. He didn't like me doing this. Something had to give. You can guess the rest. Still you never forget...

JEFFERSON Oww...

LAUREN I'm guessing you don't want to hear my story...

JEFFERSON Correct. You're a clever girl. Let's get the subject back to me.

LAUREN OK? Do you mind if I ask you a personal question?

JEFFERSON Not at all. Ask away.

LAUREN Well as a really big fan of yours...

JEFFERSON Yes...

LAUREN ...my mom...

JEFFERSON *(dejected)* Great...

LAUREN ...asked me to ask you...is that *really* your hair?

JEFFERSON Is your mom saying I'm wearing a rug? Go ahead, pull it!

LAUREN I don't like to!

JEFFERSON With Jefferson Steel what you see is what you get. Give it a tug!

LAUREN *does so.*

LAUREN Ooh!

JEFFERSON Satisfied? Now you can tell your... Mother...that Jefferson Steel has the finest head of natural hair...that money can buy!

LAUREN Impressive!

JEFFERSON You know what keeps that on? The same stuff that keeps the space shuttle together.

LAUREN You're pulling my leg?

JEFFERSON Nope honey, that's your job.

LAUREN *(laughs)* My mom said you were quite smart – even though in your films you could never keep your shirt on...

JEFFERSON Look, the parts demanded it. It was essential for the role. Why does everyone assume you don't have a brain if you look after your body?

LAUREN My point exactly. If you take care of yourself nobody takes you seriously.

Pause.

So let's have your trousers off.

JEFFERSON You're kidding?

LAUREN I need to look at your posture. Is that a problem? Do you have difficulty bending down?

JEFFERSON I'm not that old. Aaargh!

Struggles to remove trousers.

LAUREN Give me your leg.

LAUREN *begins kneading his calf.*

Your hamstring's very tight. It's referring the pain upwards. Ok – on your back...

She leans over massaging his thighs.

How's that?

JEFFERSON That feels good. Oh God. That is really good.

Suddenly the door opens, and **MARY** *is there. She sees* **JEFFERSON** *without trousers, and* **LAUREN** *on top, and it looks bad. She closes it again quickly.* **JEFFERSON** *and* **LAUREN** *are oblivious.*

More of that. Harder. Ow. That hurt! Do it again!

We hear the **FOOL**'s *song.*

MARY/FOOL

> FOOLS HAD NEVER LESS GRACE IN A YEAR/FOR WISE MEN ARE GROWN FOPPISH/AND KNOW NOT HOW THEIR WITS TO WEAR/THEIR MANNERS ARE SO APISH.

Scene Three

We are in the bed and breakfast at night. **DOROTHY** *arrives with bags of takeaway food.*

DOROTHY All part of the noble theatrical tradition – the takeaway. I am afraid Mary is at her flamenco night so you have to fend for yourself on a Thursday.

She produces tinfoil containers.

JESSICA Well I'm famished.

DOROTHY It must be nice to spend some time with your father.

JESSICA I wouldn't know.

DOROTHY Oh come on you must be proud of what he's doing here.

JESSICA I just can't get my head around it. Could he actually be doing something decent for once?

JEFFERSON *enters.*

JEFFERSON That's me. Full of surprises.

JESSICA The surprise will be if you don't screw up.

DOROTHY *starts dishing out food.*

DOROTHY So how's your back?

JEFFERSON Lauren has hidden talents. She has amazing hands.

DOROTHY *(bridling a bit)* I'm sure she has. Now, I hope everyone's hungry.

JEFFERSON So Jessica can you eat this or are you gonna explode or something?

JESSICA If you had bothered to take an interest you would know I'm not allergic to *everything*. I can eat most things. Apart from wheat and dairy products. And gluten and shellfish. And nuts, obviously...

JEFFERSON *laughs.*

JEFFERSON Obviously...

JESSICA You are supposed to feel sorry for me.

JEFFERSON Ah I was wondering what I'm supposed to be emoting in this scene.

DOROTHY *(smoothing over row)* I checked – everything is fine – it's the vegan option...

JESSICA You see Dad she's really nice. I don't understand why she's working with you?

JEFFERSON Ow!

JESSICA *(to* **DOROTHY***)* So what *is* in it for you?

DOROTHY I used to work in the theatre.

JESSICA You are so lucky...

DOROTHY I was much younger. In another life.

JESSICA So why did you quit?

DOROTHY I got married to an actor but it didn't work out.

JEFFERSON Surprise!

DOROTHY He couldn't handle the commitment.

JEFFERSON My kind of guy!

DOROTHY But I never quite managed to lose the theatre bug – and so here I am trying to direct an impossible play with an improbable cast in a delapidated barn in the middle of what you charmingly call Pigsville...

JEFFERSON Yeah, yeah, enough of the backstory. Tell me about Nigel.

DOROTHY Nigel? There's nothing to tell.

JEFFERSON *(to* **JESSICA***)* Looks like Nigel's got the hots for Dorothy...

ACT TWO, SCENE THREE

JESSICA Dad...

DOROTHY No he hasn't.

JEFFERSON I've seen him looking at you...

DOROTHY No you haven't. Besides, you're forgetting he's married.

JEFFERSON Where I come from that don't count for diddly-squat. In Hollywood the only thing that stops you fooling around is a prenup.

JESSICA Didn't stop you though, did it Dad?

JEFFERSON Only the last couple of marriages. Anyway if you want my professional opinion as a recovering serial philanderer...

DOROTHY Do tell...

JEFFERSON The truth is you're way too good for Nigel.

DOROTHY *is slightly embarrassed.*

DOROTHY If we are being embarrassing, let's talk about *your* love life.

JESSICA Urgh! Do we have to? It's all in the National Enquirer if you're interested.

JEFFERSON I'm taking a time out from women at the moment.

DOROTHY Oh really?

JEFFERSON The only woman in my life is...my daughter.

JESSICA Yeah, right.

JEFFERSON And she doesn't even like me.

JESSICA Is this where we're supposed to feel sorry for you?

JEFFERSON Touché...

DOROTHY *and* **JESSICA** *laugh.* **JEFFERSON** *takes a sip of wine.*

(To **JESSICA***)* There was a time when you used to think *I* was great.

DOROTHY What happened?

JEFFERSON *looks at* **JESSICA** *fondly.*

JESSICA I grew up.

JEFFERSON Awkward pause. During which all the characters wonder if they have just heard something heartfelt and significant.

JESSICA And cut! I am going to leave you guys to it. I better call Mom – find out how the honeymoon's going – if she's still married. Thanks for supper Dorothy.

DOROTHY Pleasure. I'll see if I can get some of these lines into his head.

JESSICA Night Dad.

JESSICA *leaves.*

DOROTHY She's a lovely girl.

JEFFERSON She is – if you're not her father.

DOROTHY So Mr. Action Hero shall we...kick some Shakespeare butt?

JEFFERSON Let's whip that sonofabard's ass!

DOROTHY *gets text out.*

DOROTHY Act One Scene Five. I'll be the Fool.

DOROTHY AS FOOL If thou wert my fool, nuncle, I'd have thee beaten for being old before thy time.

JEFFERSON/LEAR How's that?

DOROTHY AS FOOL Thou shouldst not have been old till thou hadst been wise.

JEFFERSON/LEAR O, let me not be mad, not mad, sweet heaven!

ACT TWO, SCENE THREE

Keep me in temper; I would not be mad!

DOROTHY I really think you're getting there. This could be OK.

JEFFERSON Praise indeed.

He looks at her.

Y'know something Dorothy? You're a good-looking woman but you don't make the most of yourself...you should try a bit of make up...

DOROTHY Thanks. Maybe I could borrow some of yours.

JEFFERSON smiles. He leans over to try and kiss her.
DOROTHY is tempted but avoids the kiss.

Pause.

Um...that's not in the script.

JEFFERSON I'm improvising.

He tries it again. They very nearly kiss. Then in comes MARY wearing flamenco outfit. The moment is lost.

Hey Mary did you have a good evening?

MARY *(coldly)* Not really. Enrico has never been the same since he had the accident with the castanets.

JEFFERSON I have to say Mary that you look absolutely terrific...

MARY And I have to say Mr. Steel that your opinion is no longer of interest to me.

DOROTHY What's the matter Mary?

MARY Nothing. I'm surprised to see you still up Mr. Steel given your exertions earlier.

JEFFERSON I'm good.

MARY That is a matter of opinion. Good night Dorothy.

We hear the **FOOL**'s *song performed by* **MARY** *in a flamenco style.*

MARY/FOOL
THE CODPIECE THAT WILL HOUSE
BEFORE THE HEAD HAS ANY,
THE HEAD AND HE SHALL LOUSE:
SO BEGGARS MARRY MANY.

MARY *ends this with a grand flamenco flourish.*

Scene Four

Barn rehearsal. **NIGEL** *and* **DENIS** *are helping to dress the set waiting for a rehearsal.*

NIGEL Jefferson's late as usual. One wonders whether the landlady is offering bed as well as breakfast.

DENIS You, Nigel, have a filthy mind.

NIGEL Oh come on Denis. We're men of the world. I am merely speculating about the possibility of a classic behind-the-scenes theatrical romance.

DENIS So you think Mary's shagging old Jefferson?

NIGEL Really Denis, you're very crude.

DENIS Jefferson wouldn't. He'd have told me. He's a mate.

NIGEL Correction – he's an American.

MARY *enters. Furious.*

Enter the femme fatale, stage right...

DENIS You alright Mary?

MARY I'd rather not talk about it.

DENIS What?

MARY The thing I'm not talking about.

NIGEL And where is our star?

MARY I don't know and I don't care.

NIGEL Perhaps he's having a private one-on-one rehearsal with the director?

DENIS You've got it on the brain Nige. You not getting any at home then?

NIGEL Shush. Enter Lothario – stage left.

JEFFERSON *enters with* **DOROTHY** *and* **JESSICA**.

JEFFERSON ...and I did the whole scene butt naked. True story.

DOROTHY I doubt it.

JESSICA It *so* didn't happen, Dad.

> **DOROTHY** *claps her hands to get the cast's attention.*

DOROTHY OK everyone. I have a little announcement!

NIGEL *(to* **DENIS** *and* **MARY***)* Don't tell me they're getting engaged?

DOROTHY I'm pleased to announce that the part of Cordelia will no longer be played by myself. It will be played by Miss Jessica Steel.

> *This is news to everyone including* **JESSICA** *and* **JEFFERSON**. **DENIS** *leads a round of applause.*

JEFFERSON Over my dead body...

DOROTHY Quite possibly if you have to lift me again. We can't risk your back, and I have decided I simply can't be the Fool *and* Cordelia whilst directing.

JEFFERSON But...

DOROTHY And besides Jessica has played the part before and has a particular insight into playing the daughter of a vain, spoilt, tyrant...

JEFFERSON I am not a tyrant!

JESSICA Then you won't mind if I take the role?

DOROTHY Good! So shall we go from Act One Scene Three again. Lear's dividing his time between his two daughters and neither of them are happy with the domestic arrangements.

MARY I know exactly how they feel.

> **MARY** *glares at* **JEFFERSON**...

DOROTHY OK, Mary.

MARY's *delivery is laced with extra venom.*

MARY/GONERIL By day and night he wrongs me; every hour
He flashes into one gross crime or other,
That sets us all at odds: I'll not endure it.

DOROTHY *is surprised at this performance.*

DOROTHY That's good – but maybe even a bit more anger?

MARY/GONERIL *(really letting rip)* By day and night, he wrongs me; every hour
He flashes into one gross crime or other
That sets us all at odds: I'll not endure it.

This surprises everyone with its rage.

DOROTHY Gosh! Mary I'm really feeling that anger now.

MARY I'm sorry, I can't go on with this. I don't want to be in the play any more.

DOROTHY Mary? What is it?

MARY Mr. Steel knows what I'm talking about.

JEFFERSON *(to* **DOROTHY***)* No I don't!

MARY *(tearful)* You've been a huge disappointment to me Mr. Steel!

JEFFERSON *(to* **DOROTHY***)* She's nuts.

MARY I'm sorry Dorothy. That's just how it is!

MARY *leaves in tears.*

DOROTHY Mary... Mary...come on...

MARY My final word... Goodbye!

MARY *slams the door and exits. Throughout this* **JEFFERSON** *looks genuinely mystified and annoyed.*

NIGEL Oh dear. Someone got out of bed the wrong side this morning. Or was it the wrong bed?

JESSICA *(to* **JEFFERSON***)* So what have you done Dad?

JEFFERSON I haven't done anything! In fact, I think it may be what I *haven't* done.

DOROTHY Really?

JEFFERSON *(to* **DOROTHY***)* You know Mary can come on pretty strong, and hell hath...etcetera.

DOROTHY Are you sure you're not flattering yourself?

JEFFERSON Besides, I think she may be a little jealous...

DOROTHY Of who?

JEFFERSON Of you, obviously.

DOROTHY Me?

JEFFERSON Come on. It's not *that* impossible is it?

DOROTHY Now you are flattering yourself. So what do we do now?

NIGEL Well for whatever reason, thanks to Jefferson we've just lost Goneril!

JEFFERSON So get us another one.

DOROTHY It's just not that easy.

JEFFERSON Sure it is. They'll be lining up around the block to share the stage with Jefferson Steel, Hollywood Legend...

JESSICA ...and winner of the Golden Globe for modesty.

DOROTHY Well let's see.

no changes

Scene Five

Lights come on. We see **DOROTHY** *and* **JEFFERSON** *sitting behind a trestle table.* **DOROTHY** *checks her watch.*

DOROTHY So... Where are all these people lining up around the block? It may be my eyesight but I just can't see them.

JEFFERSON Give them time.

DOROTHY I really think our time's up.

JEFFERSON We have options. There were some interesting auditions there.

DOROTHY You're even more insanely optimistic than I am.

JEFFERSON Number one was okay.

DOROTHY Enid was okay for an eighty-seven-year-old. Stretching credibility perhaps as your daughter.

JEFFERSON Number three showed promise.

DOROTHY Her obvious stage fright didn't bother you? She couldn't utter a single word? Not a line. She was even worse than you.

JEFFERSON Number two? What was wrong with number two?

DOROTHY Bernard was good – but he was, I'm sure you noticed, a man.

JEFFERSON He was interesting. It could work.

DOROTHY He had a beard.

JEFFERSON So is that it?

DOROTHY That is it.

She begins to pack up. Then a **VOICE** *is heard at the back of the theatre.*

VOICE Hello? Am I too late?

LAUREN *appears.* **DOROTHY** *raises her eyebrows.*

DOROTHY No, Lauren, please!

JEFFERSON She's a very bright girl – and kinda cute.

DOROTHY turns to JEFFERSON with a sceptical look.

DOROTHY And that's important is it – for the role of Goneril?

JEFFERSON *(serious)* I think what's really important for the role of Goneril is that she's played by the sponsor's wife.

DOROTHY *(conceding this)* Good point.

So Lauren, what are you going to do for us?

LAUREN I'd like to do the bit from Act One Scene Three, which shows Goneril's increasing coldness to her father who has moved in with her, along with his knights...

DOROTHY *(to JEFFERSON)* Someone who does their homework. Impressive. Please Lauren. In your own time.

LAUREN/GONERIL Put on what weary negligence...

JEFFERSON *(snapping shut the text)* Yeah, you've got the part!

LAUREN Really? Oh thank you! Thank you!

JEFFERSON Don't thank me, it was all Dorothy's idea.

LAUREN Whatever. And if you ever need another session...

JEFFERSON Thanks but no thanks I'm still recovering from the last one...

DOROTHY I look forward to seeing you at the next rehearsal. I'll give you a ring.

LAUREN is excited.

LAUREN Great! See you at rehearsal, Jefferson! My mom is going to be so excited that I am playing your daughter. So I guess it's ciao... "Dad"!

JEFFERSON *(feeling old)* Yeah, thanks.

As she exits, **LAUREN** *gives him a peck on the cheek. We hear the* **FOOL***'s song.*

DOROTHY/FOOL
WHEN SLANDERS DO NOT LIVE IN TONGUES,
NOR CUTPURSES COME NOT TO THRONGS;
THEN SHALL THE REALM OF ALBION
COME TO GREAT CONFUSION.

Scene Six

Rehearsal room. **DOROTHY, JEFFERSON** *and* **JESSICA**. *They are in mid-rehearsal.*

JESSICA What do you think Dorothy?

DOROTHY That's much better – now in this next scene Lear is apologising for previous wrongs. So can we have maybe... Lear kneeling in the middle of the speech?

JESSICA Sounds good to me.

JEFFERSON/LEAR Come let's away to prison;

We too alone will sing like birds i' the cage;

When thou dost ask me blessing I'll kneel down

and ask of thee forgiveness—

JEFFERSON *kneels as* **LEAR**. *It is a moving moment ruined by the entrance of* **DENIS**. *He carries a case of beer. He helps himself to a bottle.*

DENIS Beer's up!

DOROTHY Thank you Denis. I'm not sure Gloucester would be drinking this early in the morning...

DENIS Good news about Lauren, Dorothy. Great casting. Especially now the sponsor wants to maximise brand awareness.

He reads the label on the bottle.

"Lear's Bitter". You see? The beer's bitter but also Lear is bitter because of his daughter...

Another swig.

JEFFERSON We get the idea Den...

NIGEL *enters grandly.*

NIGEL Ladies and gentleman, I hate to be the bearer of bad news. But I think there is something you should see.

NIGEL *holds up the Sun newspaper, the front page of which reads "HOLLYWOOD HAS-BEEN AND BREWER'S WIFE IN SAUCY SUFFOLK SEX ROMP". Accompanying this is a big picture of* **JEFFERSON** *kissing* **LAUREN** *as we have just seen after the audition... All activity stops as everybody reads it in silence.*

JEFFERSON *(reads)* "HOLLYWOOD HAS-BEEN AND BREWER'S WIFE IN SAUCY SUFFOLK SEX ROMP" This is outrageous! *"Has-been"*? Fake news!

DOROTHY How could you?

JEFFERSON Listen Dorothy – this is all horseshit – you must know that!

JESSICA You screwed up again Dad!

DOROTHY's *mobile pings.*

DOROTHY Oh. It's Colin Bell.

NIGEL Ah, a word from our sponsor!

DOROTHY *listens intently to the call.*

DOROTHY Yes...yes... I see... OK... I understand...right...

DENIS So what did he say?

DOROTHY Basically he said we were all effing effers and we could forget our effing sponsorship and saving our effing theatre. In fact he suggested that the whole effing lot of us should go and effing eff ourselves.

NIGEL Not exactly eloquent, but heartfelt.

JEFFERSON It's not true.

JESSICA It never is, is it? You finally decided to do something worthwhile and you can't keep your pants on. I'm out of here.

JESSICA *leaves upset.*

JEFFERSON Nothing happened for God's sake!

DOROTHY So you deny it?

JEFFERSON Believe me honey, where I come from the women are so desperate for a piece of Jefferson that I have to put a padlock on my boxer shorts. If you think I porked the skinny broad in the tracksuit then you must be even crazier than the nutty bitch in the armpit motel. And in any case I'm not sure it's any of your business...

DOROTHY It *is* my business because thanks to you we have become a national laughing stock not to mention losing two of the cast and our sponsor.

JEFFERSON Big deal. At least you've still got your Lear.

DOROTHY Sadly not.

JEFFERSON What do you mean?

DOROTHY I'm afraid you're fired.

JEFFERSON You can't fire me! Nobody fires Jefferson Steel.

DOROTHY That's right. I *am* a nobody in your world and I should have known that – but you are still fired.

JEFFERSON *is in shock.*

JEFFERSON This isn't happening! I am not being blown out of a job for which I'm not even being paid!

DENIS *puts his hand on his shoulder.*

DENIS It's a cruel world, amateur dramatics.

NIGEL May I say that I am perfectly happy under the circumstances to take over the role of Lear.

To **DOROTHY**.

Poor Fool and knave, I have one part in my heart

ACT TWO, SCENE SIX

That's sorry yet for thee.

DOROTHY *(tearful)* Oh shut up Nigel! It's over. The Stratford Players are *finished*! *exit*

We hear **FOOL***'s song.* as sets hat Lx29

DENIS/FOOL
THAT SIR WHICH SERVES AND SEEKS FOR GAIN,
AND FOLLOWS BUT FOR FORM,
WILL PACK WHEN IT BEGINS TO RAIN
AND LEAVE THEE IN THE STORM.

as puts hat back Lx30
↓ barn at night

also FX18 rain

Jefferson coat on rack?

bring journalists fwd?

Nigel move throne back to SR of clothes rail

Scene Seven

The theatre. Night. There is a storm outside. **JEFFERSON** *is holed up inside the theatre. He is surrounded by empties. He has been drinking heavily and is swigging from a whisky bottle. Outside there are* **JOURNALISTS** *banging on the door and waiting to pounce... He tentatively opens the door. Flashbulbs pop. He closes it rapidly. He is on phone.*

JEFFERSON You gotta get me out of here Charlie! The paps have got me pinned down.

We hear the **JOURNALISTS** *shouting outside.*

JOURNALIST ONE *(o.s.)* How many times a night was it Jefferson?

JOURNALIST TWO *(o.s.)* Are you on viagra?

JOURNALIST ONE *(o.s.)* Come on, give us a quote!

JEFFERSON *shouts through the door.*

JEFFERSON OK here's a quote. "This cold night will turn us all to fools and madmen".

Silence from **JOURNALISTS**. *All the cameras stop for a second.*

JOURNALIST ONE *(o.s.)* Give us a more interesting quote.

JEFFERSON *(on phone to Charlie)* It's like a goddam siege Charlie...of course I didn't do it...yeah, I know I always say that but I'm a different me now...

We hear the shouting voices of the **JOURNALISTS** *outside.*

I need help Charlie...don't you give up on me... Charlie... Charlie...

The phone has gone dead. There is a bang at the door.

Leave me alone. I'm not here.

ACT TWO, SCENE SEVEN 77

JESSICA enters with her bags packed.

JESSICA *(tearful)* It's me Dad.

JEFFERSON Don't tell me Mary threw you out as well. That woman is insane.

JESSICA She didn't throw me out. I'm leaving.

JEFFERSON Don't Jessica... Me and Lauren – it's all hogwash...

JESSICA I don't want to hear it, Dad. You've let a lot of good people down...again.

JEFFERSON Even my own daughter doesn't believe me.

JESSICA I'm going back to L.A.

JEFFERSON You can't leave me. I've got nowhere to go. Everyone's deserted me.

JESSICA Goodbye Dad. My cab's waiting.

JEFFERSON No wait!

JESSICA leaves. As she does so we see a blaze of flashbulbs.

JOURNALIST ONE *(o.s.)* Jessica! What do you think about your dad being a sex addict?

JOURNALIST TWO *(o.s.)* And isn't he a bit old for all this?

JEFFERSON slumps. He sees the crate of beers and starts necking one.

JEFFERSON Who says I'm too old?

JEFFERSON/LEAR I am bound upon a wheel of fire which my own tears do...er...oh fuck it.

He has forgotten the lines and slumps down again. **DENIS** *enters through the maelstrom.*

DENIS *(shouting back at reporters)* No he didn't shag me as well. Or my mom.

JEFFERSON Denis, buddy. My saviour. You've come to rescue me.

DENIS No I haven't Mr. Steel. I've come to resign...as your entourage.

JEFFERSON But Denis. We're a team. We're crazy hombres...

DENIS I'm an ex-hombre I'm afraid. And I'm going to have to take back Mom's mobility scooter.

JEFFERSON How am I going to get to L.A. without wheels?

DENIS Perhaps you should have thought of that before you ruined everything.

JEFFERSON Have a beer Denis. I'll explain.

DENIS No thank you, Mr. Steel. I have to go and unblock a septic tank.

This is clearly untrue. There's a clap of thunder and lightning. **DENIS** *takes the scooter and drives out of the door. There is a huge commotion of hacks.*

(Shouting at **JOURNALISTS***)* Watch out before I mow you down tabloid scum!

He exits very slowly. Flash of bulbs, shouting. **JEFFERSON** *closes door behind him.*

JEFFERSON This is serious. I got to get outta here. What would Jack Finality do?

Jack Finality theme music kicks in. **JEFFERSON** *becomes the action hero and looks for an exit. He puts a chair onto the table climbs onto it and climbs up to the gallery. Down below we hear the* **JOURNALISTS** *shouting offstage.*

JOURNALIST ONE *(o.s.)* There he goes!

JOURNALIST TWO *(o.s.)* After him!

Come back Mr. Steel!

JOURNALIST ONE *(o.s.)* Come on Jefferson smash my camera – it'll make a better story!

ACT TWO, SCENE SEVEN

Sound fades as he leaves stage

JEFFERSON *is now racing round the theatre, and exits out the back. As he does so* **DOROTHY** *enters the empty theatre. She's come to pack up and sadly starts clearing the stage. She looks at* **JEFFERSON***'s suitcases.* **LAUREN** *appears.*

DOROTHY He's not here.

LAUREN Nothing happened.

DOROTHY It was all in the paper, Lauren.

LAUREN Just because it's in the paper doesn't mean it's true. In fact it usually means it isn't true.

DOROTHY In the paper there's a photograph of the two of you kissing…

LAUREN I've got a photo of me kissing Mickey Mouse. It doesn't mean we're shagging. He's old enough to be my Dad…urgh!

DOROTHY *looks mildly shocked but realises* **LAUREN** *may have a point.*

DOROTHY Mary said she saw you…

LAUREN If Mary saw anything it was me giving Jefferson physio. For his back. I was doing you a favour!

DOROTHY But the paper quotes a friend of the couple…

LAUREN *picks up the paper.*

LAUREN Yeah. And who does this "friend of the couple" sound like?

LAUREN *starts to read the article as* **NIGEL***.*

"This appalling lothario is a disgrace to the traditions of the amateur stage and has blackened the noble name of the Stratford Players".

DOROTHY *takes the paper and reads it again.*

DOROTHY Oh God. It's Nigel! I am so sorry. I have misjudged everybody. I have been a fool.

NIGEL *enters the barn dramatically.*

NIGEL Fortune, good night: smile once more; turn thy wheel! ...oh Lauren...er...

DOROTHY *hits him with the newspaper.*

DOROTHY You arse Nigel!

NIGEL What?

LAUREN *takes the paper off* **DOROTHY** *and also hits him.*

LAUREN You complete and utter arse!

DOROTHY This is your doing isn't it?

NIGEL It could have been anyone.

DOROTHY Nobody else is this pompous. "...The noble name of the Stratford Players". It's fluent Nigel-ese.

NIGEL It had to be said by someone.

LAUREN And you know for a fact that we were having an affair?

NIGEL I have an eye-witness account...

DOROTHY *(echoing* **LAUREN** *earlier)* Of Lauren giving Jefferson physio. For his back.

NIGEL Ah. But your husband doesn't seem to accept that version of events.

LAUREN That's because he's nearly as much of an arse as you are.

NIGEL I didn't come here to be insulted.

DOROTHY What did you come here for?

NIGEL I came to entreat you to change your mind. The play is the thing. It must go ahead.

DOROTHY You have got to be joking.

ACT TWO, SCENE SEVEN   81

NIGEL I've learnt all Lear's lines.

DOROTHY You really are a pathetic man Nigel. If I were Jefferson I think I might kill you.

LAUREN *(to* DOROTHY*)* Not if I kill him first.

NIGEL *retreats to the door.*

NIGEL So is that a no then?

LAUREN *picks up newspaper and chases* NIGEL. NIGEL *runs out.*

DOROTHY We'd better find Jefferson.

They both exit into the darkness. There is a clap of thunder and flash of lightning. In the blackout we hear JEFFERSON *on the run from the* JOURNALISTS *with the darkness punctured by flashlights but we do not see* JOURNALISTS.

JOURNALIST ONE *(o.s.)* There he is!

JOURNALIST TWO *(o.s.)* Jefferson are you now officially washed up?

JOURNALIST THREE *(o.s.)* Is it true you've agreed to appear on Celebrity Big Brother?

JOURNALIST ONE *(o.s.)* Will you write us a piece on media harassment?

JEFFERSON *re-appears in the gallery and climbs down onto the chair on the table and back into the barn, where he started. He turns the lights out as there is another clap of thunder outside.*

JOURNALISTS *(o.s.)* Look there's his girlfriend Lauren! Lauren!

Their voices recede as they chase her instead. It's stormy outside, but inside JEFFERSON *is dry, drunk and rambling. He gets out mobile phone.*

JEFFERSON *(into phone)* Charlie...you're the only friend I've got left... Charlie pick up the goddam phone!

Throws his mobile at the wall and slumps.

I need a drink. OK, another drink. And a smoke. You can't stop me Denis. Nor you Dorothy. Nor you Jessica. Nobody can stop me! Jefferson Steel is gonna *have* himself a cigar!

He produces a cigar, and lights it triumphantly, blowing the smoke into the air. Suddenly the siren wail of an alarm and the sprinklers come on, soaking **JEFFERSON** *who looks a bedraggled figure in the flashing red light and pouring water. Defeated, he sinks to his knees.*

JEFFERSON/LEAR Blow, winds, and crack your cheeks! Rage! blow!

You cataracts and hurricanoes, spout

Till you have drench'd our steeples, drown'd the cocks!

You sulphurous and thought-executing fires,

Vaunt-couriers of oak-cleaving thunderbolts,

Singe my white head! And thou, all-shaking thunder,

Strike flat the thick rotundity o' the world!

Crack nature's moulds, all germens spill at once

That make ingrateful man!

Suddenly, the door opens and there's **DOROTHY** *with the flashlight and an umbrella.*

DOROTHY Jefferson!

She kneels beside **JEFFERSON**, *on his knees, broken, drenched and sobbing.*

(Softly) Jefferson...

JEFFERSON/LEAR I am a man

More sinned against than sinning.

DOROTHY I know. Do you think you can walk to my place.

JEFFERSON No one walks anywhere in Los Angeles.

FX26 owl to cover movement

DOROTHY *puts a blanket over him and sits down next to him resigned to the fact that they are there for the night. Lights go down. She softly sings the* **FOOL***'s song.*

no light change

DOROTHY/FOOL

HE THAT HAS AND A LITTLE TINY WIT/WITH HEY HO THE WIND AND THE RAIN/MUST MAKE CONTENT WITH HIS FORTUNES FIT/ FOR THE RAIN IT RAINETH EVERY DAY.

LX39 darker straight into LX40 morning

Ange removes props

FX27 birds as getting brighter

cast come in as lights coming up

Scene Eight

Early morning. Sunlight streams into barn. We hear birdsong. **DOROTHY** *enters with two mugs of tea.* **JEFFERSON** *is curled up under a blanket.*

DOROTHY Good morning.

JEFFERSON God, I feel terrible.

DOROTHY *(smiling)* You look terrible. Drink this.

She gives **JEFFERSON** *a cup of tea.*

JEFFERSON I had a bad dream...

DOROTHY I'm afraid it wasn't a dream.

JEFFERSON And Jessica?

DOROTHY She left. She was very upset.

JEFFERSON/LEAR I might have sav'd her; now she's gone for ever!

JEFFERSON *sinks back in sorrow.* **DOROTHY** *puts a consoling hand on his shoulder.*

JEFFERSON Last night...did I do anything embarrassing?

DOROTHY Apart from running drunkenly all over the village, smashing a few windows and punching a photographer? No.

JEFFERSON Well *that's* a relief.

DOROTHY Oh yes. You did tell me your life story.

JEFFERSON *(groans)* Not the home-town boy from hicksville hits the bright city lights shtick?

DOROTHY Yup.

JEFFERSON And how my wives didn't understand me?

DOROTHY A lot about wives.

JEFFERSON How I've been running away from my inner demons?

DOROTHY Oh yes. We had demons.

JEFFERSON buries his head under the blanket.

JEFFERSON *(muffled)* I'm so, so sorry.

DOROTHY Please, don't be. I owe *you* an apology. In fact we all owe you an apology.

There is a lingering moment between them. They are close enough to kiss.

Drink up – we have got a cast meeting.

JEFFERSON You're kidding.

JEFFERSON groans and pulls the blanket back over his head. **MARY**, **DENIS** *enter looking a bit sheepish.*

DENIS Morning Dorothy – got your message.

MARY Dorothy – I don't know what to say.

DOROTHY Don't worry…

Enter **NIGEL** *grandiosely.*

NIGEL Greetings all… I assume Dorothy that you have thought better of your bad temper last night and have summoned us here to announce that you have had a change of heart about the play? It is of course unfortunate that our American friend has scuttled back across the pond but the show must go on…

JEFFERSON emerges from under blanket.

JEFFERSON Hey Nigel…

NIGEL *stops in his tracks, all pomposity vanished.*

NIGEL Bugger! I thought you'd gone.

JEFFERSON *advances on* **NIGEL**.

JEFFERSON You sold me out Nigel.

NIGEL No, no it was all Mary's fault.

MARY Now you've sold *me* out.

JEFFERSON You're lying Nigel.

NIGEL backs off as JEFFERSON gets closer.

DENIS Looks like someone's in for a kicking.

NIGEL turns looks desperately into the prop box and grabs a sword which he brandishes at JEFFERSON.

JEFFERSON OK Nigel! If that's the way you want it.

JEFFERSON grabs a furled umbrella. They start fencing.

DOROTHY Somebody, stop them!

DENIS Why?

An elaborate sword-fight ensues between the two men which ends with JEFFERSON dramatically disarming NIGEL. He raises the umbrella to deal the final blow as NIGEL cowers and pleads for mercy.

NIGEL Please don't hit me!

JEFFERSON then drops the umbrella, reaches out an arm and helps him to his feet. JEFFERSON steps back and looks NIGEL up and down and begins to laugh.

JEFFERSON You must have wanted that part real bad.

NIGEL It was my dream. After all my years with the Stratford Players, this was to be my crowning glory.

JEFFERSON You know what, Nigel? You play Lear. I'll be Kent. What the hell. It's only a play for God's sake.

JEFFERSON holds out his hand to shake. NIGEL is thoroughly ashamed of himself. The other members of the cast have now caught up with them and form an audience.

NIGEL Please. I can't bear the kindness. Just hit me. I'm so sorry.

The cast descend on **JEFFERSON** *and* **NIGEL**. *There is a communal feeling of repentance.*

DOROTHY We should all apologise. Mary for starting the rumour, you lot for spreading it and me worst of all for being stupid enough to believe anything I read in the papers.

The cast look at each other sheepishly.

MARY Sorry Mr. Steel...you're very welcome back at the Rectory anytime – and you can do whatever you like...not that you did do anything mind...

JEFFERSON *nods.*

DENIS Yeah, sorry Jefferson. If you ever need any shelving, u-bends, loft-lagging...

NIGEL ...or conveyancing...party wall agreement...a last will and testament...perhaps...perhaps not.

DOROTHY What were we thinking of? The Stratford Players is the one thing that keeps this village together. Even the church only holds services once a month now. This stupid theatre is all we've got. It's our community. And we were going to throw it away.

The nods of assent suggest that her speech has had its desired effect. **JEFFERSON** *turns to the cast.*

JEFFERSON I'm damned if she's going to have the big moving speech. There's something I need to say to you people.

He gets to his feet.

DOROTHY Oh dear. I think we're going to have tears.

JEFFERSON You be quiet, this is my scene.

DOROTHY It's just that if you thank all the little people I'll probably be sick.

JEFFERSON I know I can be a pain in the ass sometimes...

The cast shake their heads.

...most of the time.

The cast nod their heads.

...but until now I always thought of amateurs as "unprofessional". Nothing could be further from the truth. In fact you're the ones who deserve respect – not people like me. Because where's the glory for you guys? Where's the glamour? Where's the money? Where's the fame?

Pause.

Come to think of it...why the hell *do* you do it?

MARY It's our chance to step outside our own ordinary lives, to create something bigger than ourselves...to share in the power of theatre...

*There is a pause as the others think about **MARY**'s fine words.*

DENIS And it gets us out of the house.

They all nod in agreement. That's it. The classic British explanation for the entire motivation to create art.

JEFFERSON Whatever it is – I want to say I'd be proud, honoured in fact, if you'd let me be part of it too. Let me back in the show, and I promise I won't let you down.

*They all applaud. **DOROTHY** hugs him.*

DOROTHY Not bad. But I'm afraid the scene isn't quite over.

JEFFERSON What?

***JEFFERSON** doesn't know what she means. The door opens and the sun streams in. There in the door frame with the sun behind her is... **JESSICA**. She stands looking at her father. There's a long awkward pause.*

JESSICA/CORDELIA O my dear father! Restoration hang Thy medicine on my lips, and let this kiss

Repair those violent harms...

JEFFERSON I...don't...know...what...to...say.

DOROTHY I think you do...

JEFFERSON is stunned, but collects himself.

JEFFERSON/LEAR Pray do not mock me: I am a very foolish, fond old man...

Do not laugh at me;

For, as I am a man, I think this lady

To be my child Cordelia.

JESSICA/CORDELIA And so I am, I am.

JESSICA runs to JEFFERSON and they hug. DENIS wipes away a tear.

DENIS That's all very well but we still haven't got a sponsor.

MARY Nigel and I will simply have to go back to Colin Bell and tell him the truth.

DOROTHY Lauren tried but it's too late for that. Colin has sent out a press release disassociating his brewery from the Stratford Players and changed the name of his beer to "Colin's Bitter".

DENIS Clever. But Nigel must be minted. How much did you get for selling Jefferson's story Nige?

NIGEL *(offended by mercenary suggestion)* Nothing.

DENIS *Nothing?*

JEFFERSON You gave them "Jefferson-Steel-in Saucy-Suffolk-Sex-romp" for *free*? Now I am going to hit you!

JEFFERSON reaches for the umbrella. NIGEL looks briefly worried.

JEFFERSON *however pauses and looks into the distance.*

Wait a minute. I got a better idea... You're a lawyer Nigel, right?

NIGEL I'm a solicitor and a commissioner for oaths.

JEFFERSON I don't need any oaths but I need some soliciting.

NIGEL At your service.

JEFFERSON I want you to sue the ass off the newspapers.

DOROTHY Brilliant!

NIGEL I can't sue over a story I gave them myself. It would be unethical.

JEFFERSON *reaches for umbrella again.*

Or maybe it wouldn't. [LX 41 Centre Spot]

NIGEL *walks off into spotlight whilst the rest of the cast begin to dress the set with scenery, props and costume. Whilst this is going on we see* **NIGEL** *negotiating on phone.*

As you know I represent Mr. Jefferson Steel and it appears that your newspaper has committed a gross and indeed malicious defamation upon my client, an act of both libellus famosus and of scandalum magnatum...

You will be familiar with the quotation from the play Othello – in which, incidentally, I once played a very well received Iago – where they are speaking of reputation and Iago says:

"Who steals my purse steals trash; 'tis something, nothing; 'Twas mine, 'tis his, and has been slave to thousands; But he that filches from me my good name, Robs me of that which not enriches him, And makes me poor indeed." What does that mean in plain English? It means that according to the highest principles of English jurisprudence, I have you by the short and curlies chummy! [LX 42 Stage light]

Scene Nine

It is the opening night just before the theatre opens. The cast of King Lear *are all onstage. The costumes are much better than you would expect for amateur dramatics as are the sets we see and the props on stage.*

DOROTHY This makes a change from wearing curtains...

MARY We've never had proper costumes before.

NIGEL All thanks to my legal expertise and the generosity of the gentlemen of the press.

JEFFERSON You did good Nige. You didn't fuck up.

NIGEL Thank you. I merely pointed out to them that the damage to your reputation might be compensated by a grovelling apology and a sizeable donation to the charity of your choice i.e. the Stratford Players.

DOROTHY Very good Nigel but that's still Lear's crown you are wearing.

NIGEL Is it? I had no idea.

JEFFERSON *removes it from his head and puts it on.*
JEFFERSON *offers* **NIGEL** *a chocolate from a huge box.*

JEFFERSON Have a chocolate Nigel. First night present from the star...correction one of the stars.

NIGEL Ooh most generous...oh dear, coconut surprise...

The box travels round the cast. Enter LAUREN.

DOROTHY Lauren? What are you doing here?

LAUREN Is there a costume for me?

MARY What about Colin?

LAUREN Since the apology in the papers he feels a fool.

DOROTHY Really? He doesn't fancy playing the Fool?

She holds up motley **FOOL**'s *costume.*

LAUREN Somehow I don't think so...

DOROTHY This is very forgiving of you Lauren...

> **LAUREN** *gives her a hug. Enter* **DENIS** *dressed as* **GONERIL**.

DENIS So, does this mean I am not Goneril any more?

DOROTHY If that's not a problem.

DENIS I thought a male Goneril was an authentically period theatrical device to challenge the audience.

DOROTHY Yes – but it was more because we didn't have a female Goneril.

DENIS Fair do's.

LAUREN Do you mind Denis? I don't want to upset anyone.

DENIS Nah... Green's not my colour anyway. But I am still Gloucester?

DOROTHY Oh yes...amongst others...now off quick change...

> **LAUREN** *and* **DENIS** *go off.* **DOROTHY** *and* **JEFFERSON** *are looking offstage. Enter* **JESSICA** *looking stunning in costume.*

JESSICA Have you seen the size of the audience out there?

NIGEL Yes. It could have something to do with the fact that as part of the settlement with the newspapers I insisted that they ran free full-page advertisements for the play.

He produces paper carrying full page advertisement.

DOROTHY It says "King Lear starring Nigel Dewbury as the Earl of Kent..."

Pause.

"...with Jefferson Steel as King Lear".

ACT TWO, SCENE NINE

NIGEL Oh really – you just can't trust the newspapers nowadays.

JEFFERSON *is still looking out at audience.*

JEFFERSON That's definitely a lot of people. A lot of people come to see Jefferson Steel remember a lot of lines... Jeez.

JESSICA Dad, you are not nervous are you?

JEFFERSON Of course I am not nervous. I am absolutely terrified.

NIGEL Not a problem I could do Lear.

Pause.

Joke. I am more terrified than you are. In fact I think I am going to throw up.

DOROTHY Now we can't keep the audience waiting any longer. Everybody back stage please.

The rest of the cast exit leaving **DOROTHY** *and* **JEFFERSON**.

JEFFERSON I guess this is it. No turning back. Where's my body double when I need him?

JEFFERSON *gets out his pills.*

DOROTHY I know a better cure for stage fright.

JEFFERSON I'll try anything.

DOROTHY *leans over and kisses him tenderly.*

DOROTHY Still feeling frightened?

JEFFERSON A bit edgy.

He pulls her towards him and they kiss again for a long time. He simultaneously throws his pills offstage.

OK. Let's show 'em what a bunch of amateurs can do.

Scene Ten

Sound of trumpets. The play starts. Enter **KENT** *and* **GLOUCESTER**.

NIGEL/KENT I thought the king had more affected the Duke of Albany than Cornwall.

DENIS/GLOUCESTER It did always seem so to us: but now, in the division of the kingdom, it appears not which of the dukes he values most; for equalities are so weighed, that curiosity in neither can make choice of either's moiety. The king is coming. [Fx 29.5 trumpets]

Sennet. Enter **KING LEAR, GONERIL, REGAN, CORDELIA**.

JEFFERSON/KING LEAR Attend the lords of France and Burgundy, Gloucester.

DENIS/GLOUCESTER I shall, my liege.

Exeunt Gloucester.

JEFFERSON/KING LEAR Give me the map there. Know that we have divided In three our kingdom: and 'tis our fast intent To shake all cares and business from our age; Conferring them on younger strengths, while we unburthen'd crawl toward death. Which of you shall we say doth love us most? That we our largest bounty may extend where nature doth with merit challenge. Goneril our eldest born speak first.

LAUREN/GONERIL Sir I love you more than words can wield the matter; dearer than eyesight, space, and liberty; beyond what can be valued rich or rare; no less than life with grace, health, beauty, honour; as much as child e'er loved, or father found; a love that makes breath poor and speech unable; beyond all manner of so much I love you.

JESSICA/CORDELIA *(aside)* What shall Cordelia do? Love and be silent.

[Fx 30 fanfare]

Trumpets play. The cast, change places. The lights go down and up to indicate the progress of the play. Spotlight picks out **DOROTHY** *as* **FOOL**.

DOROTHY/FOOL They'll have me whipped for speaking true; thou'lt have me whipped for lying; and sometimes I am whipped for holding my peace. I had rather be any kind of thing than a fool! And yet I would not be thee nuncle.

Spotlight picks out **MARY** *as* **REGAN** *and* **LAUREN** *as* **GONERIL**.

MARY/REGAN This house is little; the old man and's people cannot be well bestowed.

LAUREN/GONERIL Tis his own blame; hath put himself from rest and must needs taste his folly.

Spotlight picks out **KENT** *and* **LEAR**.

NIGEL/KENT Answer my life in my judgement, thy youngest daughter does not love thee least, nor are those empty-hearted whose low sounds reverb no hollowness.

JEFFERSON/LEAR Kent on thy life no more.

NIGEL/KENT My life I never held but as a pawn to wage against thine enemies; nor fear to lose it, thy safety being motive.

JEFFERSON/LEAR Out of my sight.

NIGEL/KENT See better, Lear, and let me still remain the true blank of thine eye.

JEFFERSON/LEAR Now by Apollo.

NIGEL/KENT Now by Apollo, King, thou swearst thy gods in vain.

JEFFERSON/LEAR O Vassal, miscreant!

Spotlight picks out **JESSICA** *as* **CORDELIA** *and* **JEFFERSON** *as* **LEAR**.

JESSICA/CORDELIA O look upon me sir, and hold your hand in benediction o'er me. No sir you must not kneel.

JEFFERSON/LEAR Pray do not mock me I am a very foolish fond old man.

Spotlight picks out **DENIS** *as* **GLOUCESTER** *with his hands over his eyes.*

DENIS/GLOUCESTER All dark and comfortless. Where's my son Edmund? Edmund, enkindle all the sparks of nature, To quit this horrid act.

DENIS/GLOUCESTER *reveals a pair of googly eyes on springs. Spotlight picks out* **REGAN** *and* **GONERIL**.

MARY/REGAN Sick O sick!

LAUREN/GONERIL If not I'll ne'er trust medicine.

MARY/REGAN My sickness grows upon me.

GONERIL *screams and dies. We are now at the end of the play.* **GONERIL** *and* **REGAN** *lie dead on the floor. Spotlight picks out* **JEFFERSON** *as* **LEAR** *who strides across the stage, tears streaming down his face;* **JESSICA** *as* **CORDELIA** *limp in his arms.*

JEFFERSON/KING LEAR O you are men of stones!

Had I your tongues and eyes, I'd use them so

That heaven's vault should crack:

She's gone for ever.

I know when one is dead, and when one lives;

She's dead as earth.

JEFFERSON *has really pulled it off. He is genuinely good.*

JEFFERSON/LEAR I might have sav'd her; now she's gone for ever!

Cordelia, Cordelia...

JEFFERSON *suddenly panics as he becomes aware that* **JESSICA** *is unconscious.*

JEFFERSON *(snapping out of character)* Cordelia? Jessica? Shit! Jessica? She's unconscious! Come on say something!

NIGEL/KENT Royal Lear...

JEFFERSON Not you for fuck's sake.

Suddenly all members of the cast come alive and surround **DOROTHY** *led by* **LAUREN**.

NIGEL/KENT *(trying to stay in character)* Perchance there might be an apothecary in the establishment?

DOROTHY Shut up Nigel.

Appealing to audience.

Is there a doctor in the house?

DENIS I'll call an ambulance.

DENIS *runs off.*

LAUREN She's had an allergic reaction.

JEFFERSON Oh my God – the goddam chocolates... She's in anaphylactic shock. We'll need adrenaline, a laryngoscope and ventilatory support.

DOROTHY You're not a doctor.

JEFFERSON No, but I played one in a movie. She's going to need an emergency tracheotomy. We're going to have to go through the cricothyroid membrane.

NIGEL Are you acting now?

JEFFERSON I have no idea. But there was something about a pen...

LAUREN An epi-pen?

JEFFERSON That's it, she must have one somewhere.

DOROTHY Let's look in her bag!

DOROTHY *exits.* **LAUREN** *is taking charge, using her medical training.*

LAUREN Put her in the recovery position!

DENIS *comes back.*

DENIS The paramedics are on the way.

JEFFERSON They've got to watch out for peri-operative complications. Pneumothorax in particular.

LAUREN I expect they know that.

JEFFERSON Come on Jessica don't die on me.

He is near to tears. We hear the sound of the ambulance. **DOROTHY** *comes back with the bag.* **JEFFERSON** *tips it out all over stage and finds the epi-pen. He knows exactly what to do.*

This is it.

DENIS Are you sure you know what you are doing?

JEFFERSON I may have been struck off but I was innocent!

DOROTHY What are you talking about?

JEFFERSON Never mind. Here goes.

He removes the cap from the pen and plunges it into **JESSICA**'s *thigh. He holds it there and counts very professionally...*

One, two, three, four, five, six...

We hear the sound of the ambulance getting louder and louder. The lights go down. And up again. **DOROTHY** *comes to the front of stage and addresses the audience.*

DOROTHY Ladies and gentlemen, we are very sorry but we are going to have to close the theatre. The Duke of Gloucester insists that we run a full health and safety inspection

ACT TWO, SCENE TEN

immediately. We will of course refund your tickets. Thank you and good night.

DOROTHY/FOOL *Cast change out back*

Sings.

AND SHALL THE REALM OF ALBION/ COME TO SOME CONFUSION...

LX 44.5 scene change blues
LX 45 barn daylight
FX 32 birds
2 RH curtains
2 ~~footlights off~~
2 cloths off

Cast come on when curtains open

RH curtain
GB AP cloths
AP goblets
RH ~~GB footlights~~
RH move throne to SR of contrail

Scene Eleven

An empty stage. **JEFFERSON** *enters pushing* **JESSICA** *in a wheelchair.*

JESSICA I can walk you know.

JEFFERSON No. Doctor's orders. You need to rest. You really had me worried there.

JESSICA The doctor says I'll be fine.

JEFFERSON Well that's a relief. When I did it in the movie, the girl died.

JESSICA I'm glad you're telling me *now*.

They laugh – as **JESSICA** *gets out of the wheelchair.*

Dad you saved my life.

JEFFERSON It's the least I could do after poisoning you.

JESSICA Don't blame yourself.

JEFFERSON Please let me. It's a whole new experience.

JESSICA What's important is that you were there for me – finally.

They enter the barn where the cast are assembled. **MARY**, **DENIS**, **NIGEL** *and* **LAUREN** *give* **JESSICA** *and* **JEFFERSON** *a round of applause.*

ALL Welcome back Jessica!

NIGEL That was quite a performance. Though I say it myself I think you rather stole the show... Talk about upstaging!

JESSICA I'm just really sorry that the show's had to be cancelled...

NIGEL No matter. We can't top that as a performance.

MARY The main thing is that you're going to be OK.

DENIS We've got together all the press cuttings...thought you might like to see them.

LAUREN Not all of them, I hope.

MARY No. Just the ones about the play.

JEFFERSON You guys!

DENIS *reads from the clippings.*

DENIS "Steel Hero of Real Life Medical Drama", "Movie Star to the Rescue", "Let me through I'm an Actor".

JEFFERSON Yeah, yeah – but what did they think of my performance?

NIGEL *(reading from clippings)* Apparently you weren't...bad.

MARY You were a lot better than that! Jefferson Steel was "...startling...moving...commanding...a revelation".

JESSICA Well it's true. You were terrific.

JEFFERSON *You* were unconscious.

JEFFERSON *reads the album of clips.*

(Reading) Jeez... I haven't had reviews like this since...well I've never had reviews like this. And we didn't even get to take a bow. Bask in the warm applause. Pretend to look modest during the standing ovation...but I guess I'd better get back to Hollywood before they forget who I am, eh Mary?

MARY No one will *ever* forget you in... Raiders of the Lost Ark!

JEFFERSON Yep – I'd better get on that plane *right now*! So this really is goodbye.

NIGEL We are all going to miss you Jefferson.

JEFFERSON You're getting better at this acting business Nigel. I nearly believed you there.

NIGEL Mr. Steel, it has been...a privilege.

NIGEL *holds his hand out to shake.*

JEFFERSON Come on, Nige. Give us a hug.

He holds his arms out for a big luvvie hug-fest.

NIGEL Sorry, Jefferson you're still in England.

They shake hands.

MARY Nigel, you really are so buttoned up.

MARY *jumps on* **JEFFERSON** *and gives him a big hug and a smacker on the lips.*

Don't get the wrong idea anyone. Just saying "cheerio" …twice…

MARY *gives him another kiss.*

And once for luck…

She gives him another. **JEFFERSON** *clocks that* **DOROTHY** *is missing.*

JEFFERSON So where is Dorothy?

DOROTHY *enters breathless and excited.*

DOROTHY I'm sorry I've been on the phone.

JEFFERSON I was just saying that it's the final curtain.

DOROTHY Do you have to go?

JEFFERSON I've had an offer. Would you believe it, someone actually wants to employ Jefferson Steel?!

DOROTHY *(trying to be positive)* That's marvellous news.

JEFFERSON Yup, on the back of my performance as King Lear, they want me to play…a maverick paramedic who goes round saving people's lives. Sort of House meets The A Team.

DOROTHY A happy ending then.

JEFFERSON Kind of. I'm just sorry that…

JEFFERSON *takes her hand.*

ACT TWO, SCENE ELEVEN 103

DOROTHY It's all right. I'm a big girl. I know life isn't like a Hollywood movie...

JESSICA Well it should be.

DOROTHY The thing is it's a shame you've got to go back. Because *we've* had an offer as well.

JEFFERSON What offer?

DOROTHY We have been invited to transfer our production of Lear to Stratford...the *real* Stratford by the Royal Shakespeare Company!

NIGEL Oh my God.

Quoting from **LEAR**.

We that are young shall never see so much, nor live so long!

JEFFERSON You're not bullshitting me. This is Stratford on Avon right? As in home of the Bard?

DOROTHY I promise we are talking swans-tearooms-giftshops – the works.

JESSICA So what are you going to do Dad?

The entire cast look at **JEFFERSON** *waiting on his decision.*

JEFFERSON It's a no-brainer. Prime-time NBC with huge salary versus chickenshit Shakespeare with a bunch of amateurs?!

Pause.

Stratford here we come!

The cast applaud him.

DOROTHY You really are stark staring mad.

JEFFERSON Of course I am. I'm *Lear*!

He grabs her. They kiss. Trumpets flourish and darkness. The lights come up and the entire cast sing the **FOOL**'s *song.*

ALL
> HE THAT HAS AND A LITTLE TINY WIT –
> WITH HEY, HO, THE WIND AND THE RAIN –
> MUST MAKE CONTENT WITH HIS FORTUNES FIT,
> FOR THE RAIN IT RAINETH EVERY DAY.

Ends

FX 34 music

3x bows
LX47 dim
cast exit

LX48 preset
house lights
leaving music.

PROPERTY LIST

ACT ONE
Sets of keys – multiple sets, all with four to five keys on them
Set dressing – for theatre, old props and set lying around, including chairs, throne and sword (p6)
Luggage – set, not wheelable. One large and one smaller one (p6)
Mobile phone – possibly Blackberry – needs camera and internet (p8)
Mobile phone – iPhone (p11)
Swear box – church collection box – handmade and wood with padlock (p11)
Notepad and pen (p14)
Four chairs (p14)
Crochet (p14)
Curtains (large) – William Morris style – light wood for pole (p16)
Curtains (small) – William Morris style – dark wood for pole (p14)
Kitchen table – to fit in DSR wing (p14)
Table cloth – flowery (p14)
Condiments tray – glass jars with marmalade (p14)
Napkin holder (p14)
Stuffed fish – as dressing (p14)
Royal dressing – Coronation mugs, pictures of the Queen, royal plates (p14)
Vase of flowers (p14)
Glass of water (p15)
Box for pills – clear, including a blue pill, taken each show (p15)
Pills (p15)
Notepad and pen (p18)
Copies of King Lear – ten of Arden text (p19)
Three mugs of tea – for barn (p19)
Fake beard (p20)
Half-moon glasses – for **Jefferson** to wear (p20)
Cigar (p23)
Napkin (p25)
Mobile phone – iPhone (p25)
Briefcase (p26)
Bottle opener (p27)

Beer case – cardboard, clearly branded (p27)
Bottles of beer – 1x "Harvest Gold", 1x "Nutty Badger" and 4x "King Beer" (p27)
Mop bucket and mop (p27)
Buckets – paint buckets – with brushes (p28)
Tools – hammer, nail gun (put to someone's head), saw and upholstery hammer (p30)
Staple gun (p30)
Tool box (p30)
Sunglasses and baseball hat (p31)
Two ping pong balls (p33)
Tablet and chair (p33)
Large throne (p34)
Suitcase – one suitcase, not wheelable, retro style (p36)
Inhaler (p39)
Yellow highlighter (p40)
Pile of costumes – includes pair of curtains, ski hat with bobbles on (p43)
Ladder (p43)
Umbrella (p44)
Mobility scooter (p46)
Scooter – in case the mobility scooter doesn't work (p46)
Tesco bag – full of bottles, don't need to be many just need to make clinking noise (p46)
Laptop – also to be used for Skype conversation (p46)
Miniature pool set (p47)
Fresh flowers – cheap "garage" looking flowers. Need fresh or great fakes possibly (p47)
Giant cue card – attached to Denis's back, with King Lear lines on it (p48)
Ear piece (p49)
Walky talky (p49

ACT TWO

Pickled onion – with fork in it – placed in his eye (p53)
Bedding – flowery and pink (p56)
Bedside lamp – pink with tassels (p56)
Glasses of wine – drunk each show (p59)
Bag of takeway food – tinfoild containers, containing Indian food. Possibly eaten each show (p59)
Bottles of beer – as case used on p30 but now has a beer titled "Lear's Bitter" – drunk later (p72)

The Sun newspaper – headline –"HOLLYWOOD HAS-BEEN AND BREWER'S WIFE IN SAUCY SUFFOLF SEX ROMP" (p73)
Mobile phone (p73)
Empty bottles – including whiskey bottles, possibly the same given on p53 (p76)
Lighter – for lighting cigar (p82)
Large red tap – for sprinklers to be "turned off" (82)
Umbrella (p82)
Flashlight (p82)
Blanket (p83)
Two mugs – cups of tea – drunk each show (p84)
Towel (p85)
Wicker basket – for "costumes" to be in (p86)
Sword (p86)
Box of chocolates – eaten each show (p91)
Paper cutting – advertisement cutting (p92)
Googly eyes on springs (p96)
Epi-pen – without spring, placed in handbag (p98)
Handbag – with an epi-pen that is stabbed into Jessica's thigh each show (p98)
Wheelchair (p100)
Newspaper reviews (p101)

ABOUT THE AUTHOR

IAN HISLOP

Ian Hislop is a writer and broadcaster and has been editor of *Private Eye* since 1986. He has been a columnist for *The Listener* and *The Sunday Telegraph*, and TV critic for *The Spectator*. As a scriptwriter with Nick Newman, his work includes five years on *Spitting Image, Harry Enfield and Chums,* and *My Dad's the Prime Minister*, as well as the film and play *A Bunch of Amateurs*. He has written and presented many documentaries for TV and radio including: Radio 4's *The Real Patron Saints, A Brief History of Tax, Are We Being As Offensive As We Might Be, Lord Kitchener's Image, The Six Faces of Henry VIII* and *I've Never Seen Star Wars*. He also presented TV's *Great Railway Journeys – East to West, Scouting for Boys, Not Forgotten, Ian Hislop Goes Off The Rails, Ian Hislop's Changing of the Bard, Age of the Do-Gooders, When Bankers Were Good, Stiff Upper Lip: An Emotional History of Britain, Ian Hislop's Olden Days* and *Victorian Benefits: Workers and Shirkers*. He has appeared frequently on *Question Time* and since 1990 has been team captain on BBC's *Have I Got News For You* – which has won many awards including the BAFTA for Best Comedy 2016. Most recently he and Nick Newman wrote the critically acclaimed 2016 Radio 4 comedy drama *Trial By Laughter*. In 2016 their play *The Wipers Times* was premiered and had a successful run at The Watermill Theatre, before a sell-out tour and transfer to the West End.

ABOUT THE AUTHOR

NICK NEWMAN

Nick Newman is an award-winning cartoonist and writer. He has worked for *Private Eye* since 1981 and has been pocket cartoonist for *The Sunday Times* since 1989. His cartoons have appeared in many other publications including *The Guardian, Punch* and *The Spectator*. He was The Cartoon Art Trust's Pocket/Gag Cartoonist of the Year in 1997, 1998, 2005 and 2016. He won the Sports Journalists' Association's Cartoonist of the Year award in 2005, 2007 and 2009. In 2013 he edited the humour bestseller *Private Eye: A Cartoon History*. His scriptwriting career with Ian Hislop began with *Spitting Image*, and continued with Dawn French's *Murder Most Horrid* and *The Harry Enfield Show* – with the creation of Tim Nice-But-Dim. They also wrote the BBC1 film *Gobble* and the sitcom *My Dad's the Prime Minister*. In 2008 their film *A Bunch of Amateurs* starring Burt Reynolds was chosen for the Royal Film Performance, before being adapted for the stage at the Watermill Theatre. In 2014 their film *The Wipers Times* won the Broadcast Press Guild Award for best single drama, and was nominated for a BAFTA, before its stage adaptation and sell-out tour. Radio credits include many series of *Dave Podmore* for Radio 4 with Christopher Douglas and Andrew Nickolds, along with *Mastering the Universe*, starring Dawn French. With Ian Hislop, he also wrote Radio 4's *Gush, Greed All About It, What Went Wrong With the Olympics? The News at Bedtime* and *Trial by Laughter*.

**Other plays by IAN HISLOP AND NICK NEWMAN
published and licensed by Concord Theatricals**

The Wipers Times

Ingram Content Group UK Ltd.
Milton Keynes UK
UKHW022016200423
420514UK00010B/661